AGELATIONS

Unlocking the Secret Strategies of the Rich to Help You Succeed in Business and in Life

Other Books By Gary Lee Vincent

Nonfiction:

The Winner, The Loser

Surviving The Swine Flu

Fiction:

Passageway

Musical Releases By Gary Lee Vincent

100 Percent

Passion, Pleasure, & Pain

Somewhere Down The Road

AGELATIONS

Unlocking the Secret Strategies of the Rich to Help You Succeed in Business and in Life

Gary Lee Vincent
&
George Cunningham

First Edition

Burning Bulb
PUBLISHING

AGELATIONS
Unlocking the Secret Strategies of the Rich to Help You
Succeed in Business and in Life
by Gary Lee Vincent and George Cunningham

Burning Bulb Publishing
Post Office Box 4721
Bridgeport, WV 26330-4721

Orders@BurningBulbPublishing.com; http://BurningBulbPublishing.com

Edition ISBNs
    Softcover 13:   978-1-44213-589-5
    Softcover 10:   1-44213-589-1

First edition.
Printed in the United States of America

Library of Congress Control Number: 2009904142

Contents

Acknowledgements

I, Gary Lee Vincent, would like to extend a heartfelt thanks to the mentors of this world who poured out to me (whether they realized it or not) and helped shape the philosophies that I have today about the subjects discussed in this book.

In Real Estate, a special thanks to Ron LeGrand, Malcolm and Valerie Doney, Robert Kiyosaki, Robert Shemin, Frank McKinney, Robin Thompson, Cameron Dunlap, Dennis Quattlebaum, Richard Roop, Donald Trump, Bill Zanker (The Learning Annex), Ty Hicks, and many others too numerous to mention.

In Network Marketing, a special thanks goes out to J.J. Bradshaw, Lorie Harrell, Randy Gage, Eric Worre, Dani Johnson, and my original "Dream Team" who took a chance when I was just learning the ropes: Joseph Swick, Phyllis Vincent, Howard (De) Spurlock, Marion Spurlock, Stephanie Steinspring, Kelly and Mark Linde, Paige Paugh, Nivia Valverde, Donna Williams, Pinapple Paugh, Ed Taylor, and of course George Cunningham, the coauthor of this book. I would also like to thank Gery Craig and David Berky for their contribution.

In Wealth Psychology, special thanks go out to Jim Rohn and T. Harv Eker, with special recognition to Scott Martineau for his contribution.

I dedicate this book to You, the Reader; may your life be blessed and fruitful.

Legal Notice / Disclaimer

agile
adj.
>   1. Characterized by quickness, lightness, and ease of movement; nimble.
>   2. Mentally quick or alert.

agility
n.
> The state or quality of being agile; nimbleness.

agelation
n.
>   1. The ability to apply agile thought and multiple business methods to gain exponential success in the shortest time possible.
>   2. Synergy of success to beget greater success

Preface

"Once upon a time, I set out on a lifelong journey to
find out why the world works the way it does."
– Brian Tracy, from *The 100 Absolutely Unbreakable Laws of
Business Success*

Hello, my name is Gary Lee Vincent and welcome to our book, *Agelations: Unlocking the Secret Strategies of the Rich to Help You Succeed in Business and in Life.* I want to start off by congratulating you, the Reader, for taking action. The simple fact that you are reading this type of book tells me that you have a willingness to learn and that is the beginning of knowledge, which in turn, is the beginning of wisdom.

Part of success in any field of endeavor is the willingness to be coached. We ask that you read this book with an open mind.   As you begin this journey, I challenge you to hold one thought prevalent: "What I don't know or am unwilling to do may be the only thing keeping me from my dreams."

Think about that for a moment. What is it you don't know or are unwilling to do? We all have certain beliefs, certain thoughts.   These 'algorithms' program our reality and in essence, shape our outcomes in life.

Understand this, Dear Reader, that what YOU believe to be TRUE may only be true for you; and if you have not accomplished what you deeply desire in life, it may be a result of your beliefs.

Put your head around that for a moment. Could it be that you are programming your own financial thermostat based on what you are *thinking* and what you have been taught by *others* to believe?

If that is the case (which, by-the-way, is often the case), then it is reasonable to *believe* that you can be reprogrammed with thoughts that will edify you and bring you closer to what you desire in life.

That is why we start this book off by saying that you need to be coachable and have an open mind to receive what it is that George and I are going to be teaching you. There is a good possibly that some of the things we say will make you uncomfortable. That's okay.

This book is not designed to make you feel good; there are plenty of those out there in any Self-Help section of your local bookstore. In fact, you might find yourself disturbed as you read this, because ultimately, you are responsible for where you are right now *and* where you are going.

In his book, *The Power of You!: How YOU Can Create Happiness, Balance, and Wealth,* Scott Martineau puts it like this:

"To achieve total freedom in life there are certain things that must be understood. For starters, a person MUST take complete responsibility and accountability for their selves: for their actions, their thoughts, their goals, their passions, their mistakes, their financial situation, their spirituality and their happiness. Without total responsibility and accountability total freedom can never be fully achieved."

Therefore, Dear Reader, I challenge you to feel what is going through your mind as we present the material; also, objectively question what you hear from others: are they imposing their belief system on you? In other words, think and use your brain... for a change (both meanings intended.)

This book is written by two people, George Cunningham and me, Gary Lee Vincent. It is written in the first person from both of us, as we share our life experiences and observations on the given topics.

My words will be written in this **Antique Olive font.** George's will be written in Century Gothic font, so that you can distinguish who is speaking.

On behalf of both of us, we thank you for taking the time to read, and hopefully implement, this book and its teachings. As we start, keep this in mind...

Thoughts lead to feelings,

feelings lead to actions,

and actions lead to results.

Are you ready for results? Then let's get started!

I. Introduction

> "Faith is taking the first step when
> you can't see the whole staircase."
> – Martin Luther King, Jr.

Who are we and why should you read this book?

GC: My name is George Cunningham and I am the founder and President of Agility Inc. of Nevada. I founded Agility Inc. in order to be the leader in providing the small business entrepreneur with the skills and tools needed to succeed both professionally and personally.

To this endeavor, I bring my education in business management and several years of experience in managing personal finance and information technology resources.

I chose to collaborate with Gary in writing *Agelations* in order to bring my personal experiences with various business models to the reader in hopes that he/she will learn from my successes and avoid the pitfalls that led to my failures. In this way, I hope to do my part in improving the lives of others.

♦♦♦♦

GV: I have a diverse history in many different fields. In 1992, I founded Vincent Record Company and the VINCE record label to promote independent musical works.

I have a Ph.D. and Master of Science Degree in Computer Information Systems and have been an IT consultant on several business websites. I also hold a Bachelor of Science Degree in Business Administration Management and Psychology.

In 2004, I founded Vincent Inter-national Properties, Inc. to manage and pursue real estate investments. In 2006, I began investing in self-storage facilities and am presently the owner of multiple properties in West Virginia and Ohio.

The idea for creating *Agelations* came in 2007. I was on a real estate investor cruise where a fellow investor introduced me to a network marketing opportunity. Though I will admit that my work schedule left little time for another 'business', I couldn't help but be intrigued.

This gentleman was a major stake-holder in California wind farms and also invested in self storage facilities, as I did. He was a multimillionaire that had retired from real estate. This gentleman was not peddling anything, nor did he have a need. He showed a genuine interest in this company and its business model, so much so, that I asked him for additional information and eventually purchased a position in the business.

Over the weeks and months that followed, I immersed myself in learning about network marketing; what it was and what it was not. I tried a few different things ranging from home meetings, conference calls, seminars, etc. There were peaks and valleys throughout this entire process.

What I liked about the opportunity was it allowed for a way for anybody to get started with very little money with a product line that was excellent.

What I didn't like was that many people would purchase a business package with a genuine intention of wanting to be successful only to later lose focus or become distracted with life's other concerns. Ultimately these individuals would become discouraged and leave the business.

Later that year, I formed Agel Dream Team, LLC, to focus on my immediate group and on growing my network marketing business in a traditional sense. I listened to concerns and followed the progress of many in my group. As I witnessed people coming and going from the business, I decided that a more congruent approach would be needed for people to attain success.

I noticed that there were different schools of thought on how one should operate a network marketing business. I also noticed that there were rock stars in each model, thus any given method could arguably produce success.

However, I did not see this as being the case for the majority of individuals. I saw many people trying hard early on, and then dropping off. If you are in network marketing, then perhaps you have witnessed this.

In my real estate endeavors, particularly my self storage businesses, I developed systems of automation to do some of the grunt work for me (such as automatic rentals, websites, phone centers, etc.) and knew that there had to be a way to combine expertise and technology to achieve automation that will build success. It is these findings that I share with you in this book.

II.   Paradigms of Wealth

Types of Wealth

GV: Before I get into the details of how to become prosperous, it may be a good idea to define what being "wealthy" means to you. I have personally witnessed extremes on both ends of the spectrum.

I have seen people with millions who were too stressed out to enjoy life and seen people that were destitute, living in shacks, but were happy. In these extreme circumstances, many people not looking *inward at themselves* might adopt the stereotype that being rich financially means that you will be unhappy, or that you must neglect your needs or feel badly if you have more than the neediest of people.

This is an incorrect way of thinking. Happiness towards one form of prosperity does not equal happiness in all areas of life for all people. I have seen rich people extremely happy just as I have seen poor people who were bitter and terribly unhappy. In this world of 6 billion plus people, there are all types.

What's God Got To Do With It?

Human beings are spiritual creatures, whether we choose to admit it or not. There are forces at work outside the realm of our comprehension and as soon as you understand this, you can allow these forces to work for you instead of against you.

Regardless of whether you agree with me on this point, I believe that there is a God who created the universe and has given each of us specific skills and put us in specific circumstances. Not all are created equal, and like it or not, that's just a fact of life.

We are each given free will to do what we wish and to that extent, we determine what we make of our lives. **Based on our beliefs, we ultimately determine our own level of wealth.**

Our wallet, our health, our spirituality is all a result of what degree of *worth* we have towards that area of life. Do you believe you are *worthy* of having more?

In the first book of Chronicles, the first three chapters and part of the fourth read like a family tree. It's terribly boring and most people reading through the Bible are likely to skip it (and maybe the whole book entirely).

However, the genealogy breaks off at Verse 10 to show where one person, Jabez, asked God for more. He asked God to expand his territory and God granted his petition. Verse 11 picks up the genealogy report again.

Bruce Wilkinson created a bestselling book, *The Prayer of Jabez*, completely around this single verse. But he has a point, God gives more to those who seek it.

But it's not simply enough to ask God for more. We must show that we are *worthy* stewards of what we have so that God can *trust* us with more.

God wants us to have more, but are we worthy? What did you buy last payday? Here, let me give you another way to look at this...

The Parable of the Talents

The Parable of the Talents  is a parable told by Jesus in the book of Matthew, Chapter 25, verses 14-30. It was told to illustrate an aspect of the nature of the Kingdom of Heaven.

The parable tells of a master who was leaving his home to travel, and before going, gave his three servants different amounts of money.

On returning from his travels, the master asked his servants for an account of the money given to them.

The first servant reported that he was given five talents, and he had made five talents more. The master praised the servant as being good and faithful, gave him more responsibility because of his faithfulness, and invited the servant to be joyful together with him.

The second servant said that he had received two talents, and he had made two talents more. The master praised this servant in the same way as being good and faithful, giving him more responsibility and inviting the servant to be joyful together with him.

The last servant who had received one talent reported that he buried his talent in the ground for safekeeping, and therefore returned the original amount to his master.

The master called him a wicked and lazy servant, saying that he should have placed the money in the bank to generate interest. The master commanded that the one talent be taken away from that servant, and given to the servant with ten talents, because everyone that has much will be given more, and whoever that has a little, even the little that he has will be taken away.

It is interesting how the term 'talent' can have two meanings, both valid here. On the surface, it can simply mean to be a better steward of the finances with which you have been entrusted. It can equally mean to use your abilities rather than bury them.

Biblical Misconceptions

Agelations is by no means a religious work, nor was it intended to be. However, I see so many people misquote the Bible in relation to money that I want to stop and address it before we go any further.

If you have heard some of these quotes taken out of context, perhaps you too are under a false impression that to be wealthy financially means to be evil or that God would hate you. This is preposterous, so let's get into my interpretation on these common thoughts. Take it for what it's worth.

"Money is the root of all evil." It is amazing how one little word makes all the difference in the world. In the first book of Timothy, Chapter 6, verse 10, the Bible actually states, "The *love* of money is the root of all sorts of evil."

If your only purpose to get rich is because you love money, you will have a lot of grief. Gold without God will leave you empty.

However, if you want to get rich to have a better life and use your blessings to help others, then you are not in love with money, but having a desire for a better good.

When you are faced with challenges, you can go forward in faith knowing that a greater purpose serves you, not just a bigger checking account. This attitude is not evil.

"A rich person will not go to heaven." I can see how this one could easily be used by religious leaders to extort money from their congregation. In fact, it was Jesus himself who said, "It is easier for a camel to go through the eye of a needle, than for a rich man to enter into the kingdom of God." (Matthew 19:24)

So, are we left with a paradox? Not exactly. If a person takes this phrase by itself, then you could put this book down and go about being broke for it would make no sense to strive for riches as it would conflict with the positive outcome of one's soul.

However, I think it's best to see the ***entire*** text so that you read what was literally said *in context* and I'll comment afterwards (taken from the Holy Bible, New International Version):

16

Now a man came up to Jesus and asked, "Teacher, what good thing must I do to get eternal life?"

17

"Why do you ask me about what is good?" Jesus replied. "There is only One who is good. If you want to enter life, obey the commandments."

18

"Which ones?" the man inquired.

Jesus replied, " 'Do not murder, do not commit adultery, do not steal, do not give false testimony,

19

honor your father and mother, 'and 'love your neighbor as yourself.'"

20

"All these I have kept," the young man said. "What do I still lack?"

21

Jesus answered, "If you want to be perfect, go, sell your possessions and give to the poor, and you will have treasure in heaven. Then come, follow me."

> **22**
>
> When the young man heard this, he went away sad, because he had great wealth.
>
> **23**
>
> Then Jesus said to his disciples, "I tell you the truth, it is hard for a **24** rich man to enter the kingdom of heaven. Again I tell you, **it is easier for a camel to go through the eye of a needle than for a rich man to enter the kingdom of God."**
>
> **25**
>
> When the disciples heard this, they were greatly astonished and asked, "**Who then can be saved?**"
>
> **26**
>
> Jesus looked at them and said, "**With man this is impossible, but with God all things are possible.**"

If you read this at face value, it basically says that it is impossible to enter the kingdom of God, whether you are rich or poor, but with God, all things are possible.

On the other side of the coin, I have also seen religious scholars make an analogy of something called "Needle's Eye."

The needle gate was a narrow gate thought to have existed in ancient Jerusalem. It was an entry-point to the city and was built like the eye of a needle and so low that a camel could pass only if it entered kneeling and unencumbered with baggage.

The lesson would then be that an eternal inheritance awaits those who unburden themselves of sin, and in particular, the things of this world.

Also, kneeling represents submission and humility, which are required to enter into heaven.

Although there is no historical evidence that such a gate ever existed during the time frame of Jesus' ministry, it is a widely used alternative interpretation of the quote.

My thoughts: take the text for its literal meaning; rich or poor; you need God's help to get to heaven. In my belief system, God's help was Jesus Christ, yours may be different. So, if being rich or being poor isn't necessarily going to get you to heaven, we might as well look at how to be rich versus being broke, leave the spiritual work to the Lord and use our wealth for the greater good of mankind. Sound good?

♦♦♦♦

GC: I believe that Gary makes many valid points in his assessment. Wealth truly does mean different things to different people. Is the attorney that spends 12 hours a day researching cases for an upcoming court date truly wealthy and happy? Is the person that is on call 24 hours a day, seven days a week, free to do as he/she pleases?

These are questions of choice and can only be answered by the individual. I would like everyone that reads this book to answer the following question:

Have you truly taken the time to determine what makes you happy and content?

If not, then this should be your very first step. Personally, I have found that true monetary wealth simply allows an individual the freedom to do as he/she likes. My true measure of wealth is a direct correlation to the level of personal satisfaction in one's life. This is the ultimate intangible and cannot be measured in dollars and cents.

How the Rich Think

GV: I believe that we are all a product of our environment; and to that extent as it relates to our past, we have little control.   What we do control however is what we become.   We control whether or not we will allow our past circumstances to dictate our future successes or failures.

The universe is driven by cause and effect. Many people think that if they work hard in a good job that they will become wealthy; that they will get that promotion and that everything will be fine.   This is not how rich people think.

What many do not realize is that if you are doing the same thing day after day, you can expect the same or very similar results that you've been getting. The definition of insanity is doing the same think over and over and expecting a different result. Think about that one.

Building on that, it can be deduced that you must think in a way that will bring wealth to others, which will in turn bring wealth to you. More specifically, you are paid according to what value you bring to the world.

Many of you reading this book have had opportunities pass you by because you were not aware that they were opportunities, or perhaps you knew they were opportunities and choose to ignore them.

That being said, I could further deduce that being in the right place at the right time is not enough: you need to be the right *person* at the right place at the right time.

But how can you be the right person? It all starts with awareness. You made the right choice by reading this book, as it is our intention to make you aware of several things that may be holding you back from the success you deserve.

Consider your mind a sponge: reading books such as this, continuing your education in non-traditional ways, attending seminars, etc. are all positive steps towards getting your awareness expanded.

◆◆◆◆

GC: I would like to give a real world example that further reinforces the point that Gary is making. Wolfgang Amadeus Mozart is widely considered to be one of the greatest classical composers in history and justifiably so.

He was a very talented individual that most would describe as a true musical prodigy. **But was he really?**

Let's examine his childhood history. Mozart began writing music by the age of six. Was his first masterpiece written when he was 6, 7 or even 10?

No. It was written when he was 21. What can we infer from this examination?

Mozart was a gifted classical composer that honed his abilities for nearly 15 years before writing his first masterpiece. He was talented **AND** he was willing to spend thousands of hours over a 15 year span to improve and perfect his techniques.

Thus, it helps to have a wealth of talent, but this is not the entire story. It takes the willingness to succeed and the desire to commit the time needed to become a master.

You have demonstrated the willingness to succeed by purchasing this book. Will it take 15 years to master its contents? No. Gary and I will be your guides to financial freedom and together we will provide you with the tools required to become your own master.

◆◆◆◆

Your Financial Baseline

GV: Second, you need to critically analyze yourself. What is your financial baseline? What I mean by 'financial baseline' is not how much money you have in the bank, but rather what level of wealth are you capable of handling? This is not an easy answer.

Most people have a financial baseline that drives them. No matter how little or how much money they earn, they usually have a similar lifestyle throughout their life.

The person who is broke or living paycheck to paycheck will typically live from paycheck to paycheck regardless of his or her job. When they do get a raise, they increase their lifestyle just enough to stay where they are financially and are still living paycheck to paycheck.

Conversely, those who are wealthy can have their wealth taken from them and in a very short time have it back.

I have heard countless stories of people like Donald Trump and Charles Givens who have had wealth, lost wealth, and got it back again. See, the financial baseline of these individuals is set to RICH.

They are attuned to the opportunities the world provides and can rebound from financial disaster faster and more efficiently than many other people just because of their financial baseline. They may have temporarily lost their money, but they did not lose their cognitive process – their ability to think and rebuild their wealth.

I would contend that most people live unfulfilled lives. I would go out on a limb to say that not living up to one's full potential creates great unhappiness.

Although many would claim to be victims of their circumstances, they themselves are the cause of their unhappiness. They live a careless life, paying no attention to the details around them: they get up day after day, go to their boring job, come home, watch TV, go to bed, get up the next day and repeat.

They do this over and over until one day they 'wake up' at retirement wondering where the years gone by. With sad remorse, they say to themselves: "why life couldn't have been just a little bit better."

Reader, every life is important. God did not place you here to simply go through your life on cruise control. You are here for a reason and you must wake up to find it.

◆◆◆◆

GC: Gary makes some interesting points in this dialog. How much wealth can you really handle? Answer this question:

Have you ever dreamed of winning the lottery?

Let's face it, most of us would answer 'yes' to this question, but consider this: If you were raised in a middle or lower income environment, are you truly prepared to handle this new found wealth? You could easily find yourself overwhelmed with managing your new financial windfall.

As a practical example, every day I read in the newspaper about highly skilled and paid professional athletes that find themselves in trouble either professionally or legally. I am not trying to say that all athletes have this problem but many do.

Often, their new found financial freedom manifests negatively and basically ruins their life. Was it the money or fame, or was it something deeper in their psychology that was the root of the problem?

So I say this again because it bears repeating: "How much wealth can you really handle?" This is indeed a very valid question.

The Parable of the Fig Tree

GV: The Gospel of Mark gives an account of Jesus withering a fig tree. He came to it one day when he was hungry and there was  nothing on it but leaves. Although it wasn't the season for the tree to bear fruit, Jesus cursed the tree. Consequently, it no longer bared fruit even when the season came.

Many possible meanings can be taken from the parable, but for this book, I believe the story is analogous to living your life in an unfruitful way to the point that when it is the season to reap your success, you have nothing to show.

More specifically, we are not too different from the fig tree. Our past circumstances, current attitudes, and mental outlook on life create the roots of which our tree of life is based.

Thus our 'figs' will either grow and ripen at the time of harvest or our lives, like the tree in the parable, will be withered and barren.

Security Versus Financial Freedom

I think before I go any further that I need to clarify a very big misconception that many people have. Many believe that financial security and financial freedom are the same thing when, in reality, they are opposites of each other.

Think about it this way: how free is a person in prison? Or to put it another way, how *secure* is he? Have you ever thought that your "safe, secure job" is actually a different form of prison that is actually contributing to your financial problems more than helping you attain financial freedom?

Now, I'm not saying that you should all go out and quit your jobs right after reading this. What I am saying is that you need to start making concrete plans to get you out of the rat race and into a more affluent financial status.

In other words, you need to **plan your prison break!**

In today's tough economic times, many people are discovering that the jobs their parents relied on are no longer a secure means of earning a living. Just pick up any newspaper or turn on the TV and you will see companies left and right shutting their doors or outsourcing their labor to foreign countries that can do it cheaper and with less government regulations. This is just a fact of life.

Therefore, you need to begin making that mental shift and start doing the activities that will *increase your financial baseline*.

Traditional Education –
Breeding a Society of Dependents

Now for my next controversial point: many people are educated to be poor. I have earned a Ph.D., Masters, and B.S. degree from traditional educational institutions. Although each helped me attain a better paying job, my first million dollars was made using specific skills I learned non-traditionally by learning to invest in real estate from Ron LeGrand.

I've come to believe that everybody should at least go through school. However, they should go though it with an awareness that it does not stop there. **Traditional education and financial education are two distinct and different things**. You cannot get ahead without a solid financial education on top of your traditional schooling.

There is a serious lack of financial literacy in today's society. People are school smart and broke. Do we blame the professors or the institutions? Maybe they both share some responsibility.

Most professors do not make that much money and are only passing down what they have learned to their students. They can teach you to get a better paying job, but most cannot teach you to be rich.

The schools are equally guilty because they mandate curriculums to 'get hours in' that often have no grounding in the real world – especially in the areas of wealth creation.

So where am I going with all this? Reader pay attention: be very careful who you listen to for financial advice. Is the person living the lifestyle that you are wishing to attain or are they simply living a lower or middle class existence?

You cannot expect to gain the skill sets you need to succeed from someone who hasn't attained that for his/herself. That is why I don't use a financial advisor; I ask them if they have more money than I do and if the answer is no, then I would be remiss to take their advice. Do keep this in mind: brokers are called brokers for a reason.

So where can you get sound financial advice? At the end of this book, we will provide you with a list of references and websites that you can use to further your financial education. I would strongly suggest you diligently pursue your financial education further through these non-traditional means until you have, in fact, re-established your financial baseline to be much higher than it currently is now.

Willingness to Take Risks

There is a lot that can be said for the cliché, "No risk, no reward." I also like how A. E. Hotchner put it: "I would rather fail in an attempt at something new and uncharted than safely succeed in a repeat of something I have done."

One must be willing to move from his or her comfort zone and take risks. Now, I'm not saying that one should take large financial risks such as gambling his life savings or retirement on some risky new IPO stock.

What I am saying is that one should be willing to look at new business opportunities, possibly pick up a piece of investment real estate, or engage in an entrepreneurial endeavor they might not otherwise do.

Also, learn to be a good steward of your money. Mimic the rich in terms of watching their behaviors, *especially how they make money work for them.*

Do not mimic any bad habits, such as living above your means or spending money foolishly just to copy what a rich person down the street may be doing. Let me give you some examples...

What Rich People Buy on Payday

My friend J.J. Bradshaw had a cute video on his network marketing website that depicted a scenario of what rich people buy with their money. I have also seen a similar analogy in Robert Kiyosaki's *Rich Dad* series, which I highly recommend.

Anyway, to put a very complex subject in a nutshell, poor people work for money and rich people have their money work for them. Poor people spend their money on things that continue to cost them money and rich people spend their money on things that make them money.

Many people strive to buy a new house or new car. Though there is nothing wrong with this, these purchases will inhibit your ability to get rich if you are purchasing them with money earned from a job.

Let me clarify: are you trading hours for dollars? If so, how much time can you possibly put in to earning a living: 40 hours, 60 hours?

What I am trying to get at is this: you can only work so long. Each of us only has 24 hours in a day. The magic has to happen in this finite and limited resource.

Now, let's take the above example of buying a new car. A non-financially educated person would go out and get a loan to buy the car. Let's say the car has a $300.00 per month payment. If this person worked a $10.00 an hour job, 30 hours of his first 40 hour work week in each month would already be spent in the car payment!

A rich person would ask himself: what could I buy that would make the car payment? They may go out and look for a house that they could purchase that would have a similar payment to the car, and then rent the house for $600.00 per month. The renter would make both the mortgage payment and the car payment with the rent. Has a light bulb come on yet?

Three Distinct Paths to Financial Freedom

In the chapters that follow, we are going to take a look at three areas that are proven models of creating wealth: Real Estate, Information Marketing, and Network Marketing.

There are literally thousands of ways to get rich, however we have chosen instead to focus on ones that have worked for us and that we feel can work for you too.

Using any one or a combination of the three will give you a greater chance at achieving financial freedom and the lifestyle you desire, and the best part: they all can be ran as a business from home!

But first, we are going to look at one of the biggest secrets the rich use to stay rich: the tax code!

I would like to close this chapter with a quote from athlete Alberto Salazar: "If you want to achieve a high goal, you're going to have to take some chances."

III.   Tax Secrets of the Rich

> "By a continuing process of inflation, government can confiscate, secretly and unobserved, an important part of the wealth of their citizens."

> "The avoidance of taxes is the only intellectual pursuit that still carries any reward."
> – John Maynard Keynes

GV: If there was one piece of advice that I could give that would pay for this book hundreds of times over, it would be to start a home-based business. While most people start a business to be their own boss, there are several more important reasons that I wanted to bring to your attention.

This book will introduce you to a variety of different businesses; some of which can be started for just a couple hundred dollars. Having your own business can literally save thousands of dollars each year in the form of deductions!

What most people fail to comprehend is this: even if your business doesn't end up in the Fortune 500 list of top earning companies, you will still come out ahead through the tax credits from owning the business. And who knows, you might end up making far more this way than the cost of the business itself!

◆◆◆◆

GC: I would like to interject some advice at this point that will save our readers major headaches later. You must treat your endeavor as a business. You simply cannot start a home-based business or join a network marketing company, do nothing, and expect to be rewarded with numerous tax deductions. Simply starting a business with the intent to take deductions is illegal. You must be engaged in the business with the intent to make a profit.

THE BURDEN OF PROOF IS YOURS. YOU MUST PROVE TO THE IRS THAT YOU ARE ENGAGED IN A BUSINESS ENTERPRISE AND NOT A HOBBY OR A MEANS TO GENERATE DEDUCTIONS.

For most people involved in a home-based business, the sheer number of tax savings alone is worth the startup costs. Consider this question:

Are you losing money by not starting a home based network marketing business?

This is a simple, straight forward question. Would it surprise you to know that more than 70% of the people that we surveyed answered incorrectly!

♦♦♦♦

The Educated Few

GV: If you are an employee who is working for someone else and do not have a business of your own, you are paying unnecessary taxes. Most Americans are in this category and are what I call "uneducated" in regards to paying taxes.

It is important for you to understand this: **there is a set of tax rules for the W-2 wage earners that is different than those with small businesses.**

Those in the W-2 system are taxed on their entire income and are forced to survive on only part of their salary. These taxes can be as high as 50%! On the other hand, the rich often only pay single digit taxes, sometimes as low as 4% - 5%.

Business owners are part of the "educated system" and can deduct things like a home office, their car(s), travel, and specific meals and entertainment. An entrepreneur can reduce his/her tax bill literally by thousands simply by converting their largest expenses into business expenses eligible for a tax deduction.

Ask yourself this: which is better for you; living on only 50% of your income or 96%? Ultimately, it is your choice but if you are like me, I find that I can put this excess money to much better use building sustainable wealth versus giving it to the government.

There are over 300 deductions that are available to you as a business owner. Though we are not going to cover them all here, we will give you some to think about.

Types of Deductions

Home Office. If you have a space in your home that is dedicated to your business and nothing else, then you can claim the home office deduction.

How do you calculate this? Measure your work area and divide by the square footage of your home, and that percentage is the fraction of your home-related business expenses, including rent, mortgage, insurance, electricity, etc., that you can claim.

Another way to do it is to divide the home office room by the total number of rooms (i.e., 1 room divided by 6 rooms total in a house would give you 16.7%, and this would be the amount of home expenses you could write off for your home office.)

GC: If you own your home, you have a gold mine.

Designate an area of your house as an office.

You can deduct a portion of the following:

- Utilities
- Business Equipment
- Home owners insurance
- Local housing fees, if applicable
- Landscaping
- Roofing
- Siding

- Painting
- Any remodeling within reason. *(They will accept a ceiling fan, but not a $10,000 crystal chandelier)*
- Internet connection
- Etc...

GV: Mileage. If you drive for business, you can realize some big write offs here, but you'll need to keep good documentation. For starters, keep a notebook (I prefer a day planner) in your vehicle to record the date, mileage, tolls, parking costs and the purpose of your trip.

At the end of the year, you have two choices:

METHOD 1: You can total the mileage and add in the tolls and parking to calculate your deduction. Once you have your mileage total, multiply it by a certain amount. This amount is defined by the IRS and changes from year to year. For example, in 2008, it was 50.5 cents per mile.

GC: On July 1, 2008, the standard rate allowance for business related mileage was increased to .585 cents per mile!

Burden of proof: Keep a log book in your car and state the beginning and ending mileage of every business trip you take as well as a running total. State the reason for the trip and list the other individuals that were involved.

All miles driven while engaged in a business related service can be deducted. Travel to meetings, training seminars, team members' homes, etc...

METHOD 2: You can measure your business usage against your personal driving and deduct that portion of your auto-related expenses, remembering to include gas, repairs and insurance. If you are leasing, include those payments. If you are buying the car, factor in the interest on your loan and depreciation on your vehicle.

If your company's office is at your house, you're in luck: you can deduct the entire business-related mileage, from the time you pull out of the driveway until you return home. If your business is not home-based, your mileage meter starts at your first business-related destination and ends at your last. You can't include the drive to and from home.

Travel. The cost of travel is 100 percent deductible, as are costs associated with life on the road (dry cleaning, rental cars and tips).

GC: How in the world can you make a vacation deductible?

Make it a business trip.

Remember to document all this. On the flight to the destination, leave one of your company's promotional items and your business card in the magazine compartment of the seat in front of you.

Try to talk about your business to the person beside you. The flight is deductible.

Leave a business card with the taxi driver or rent a car during the business trip. It becomes deductible.

At the hotel, leave promotional materials in the room, with the magazines in the lobby, or in the lobby display showing fliers for local areas of interest.

Leave a business card each time you dine in the restaurant and maybe talk to the waiter/waitress about the business opportunity. Talk to one person a day about the business. Document it.

The Company Meeting. The tax code requires that you update your formal corporate documents annually. This includes keeping accurate financial records, corporate resolutions and minutes, etc. As the owner of your business, you can combine your annual meeting with a vacation and make the entire trip deductible. You can also bring your family along as well.

Meals and Entertainment. You can deduct 50 percent of your meals while traveling. Save your receipts and just be careful not to deduct the full 100% when doing your taxes.

GC: Keep your receipts! Sign on the back and state the reason for the meeting & with whom you met.

With a network marketing company, for example, virtually anyone can be a client or a prospective client. Additionally, you can deduct all meals within a 24 hour period of a business meeting due to possible travel to and from the meeting. I think it is easy to see the possibilities.

There are also ways to make entertainment expenses deductible. The trick is to entertain a client or a team member and discuss business during the event, and document what was discussed during the meeting.

Take deductions for:

Movies, Baseball games, Concerts, Vacations, Etc.

The list is endless.

The Company Gym. The IRS won't let you deduct the price of your gym membership, but you can deduct the cost of gym equipment. Keep this in mind the next time you are watching an infomercial and see a piece of equipment you've just got to have (for the business).

Insurance Premiums. If you are self-employed and paying your own health insurance premiums, these costs are 100 percent deductible. You also can include some of the premiums you pay for long-term care insurance for yourself, your spouse or dependents.

Retirement Contributions. Your company can establish its own retirement plan, such as a SEP-IRA or Keogh. It can include you, your spouse and your children. The nice part is these are deductible.

Seminars. Your company can pay for the cost of educational seminars, even if they have nothing to do with your current business! So, for example, let's say you want to purchase our home study course or attend a training event, it's 100% deductible!

Social Security. This is a double-edged sword. If you're self-employed or starting a small business, you have to pay double the

Social Security contributions you would as an employee. That's because federal law requires the employer pay half and the employee pay half. Self-employed workers are both, meaning the total will equal 15.3 percent of your net profits.   But, on the positive side, you can deduct half of the contribution on your 1040.

Telephone.   Since the IRS assumes that you will have a phone in your house anyway, regular fees and charges don't count toward your deduction. But if you have a second line installed and use it only for business, all of these charges are deductible.

Achievement Awards. Each year, your company can give away three separate awards to its employees. Each of these awards is worth $1,600 per year in kind; however it can't be in the form of money. What this means is you can't write the employee a check for $1,600, but rather, you can present him or her a gift (in kind). These gifts can range from just about anything: TVs, sporting goods, furniture, etc. – anything but cash.

The first gift is for longevity. This is reserved to companies in existence for five years or more. You can present the gift to your longest standing employee and if you are the only employee of the company, then this would be you.

The second gift is for safety. This gift is typically reserved for companies in a risky business such as construction. If you are a real estate rehabber, this would qualify.

The third gift is for excellence in sales. You can award your best salesperson this award based on their stellar performance during the prior year.

Child Labor. Here's a novel idea: how about instead of paying your kids an allow- 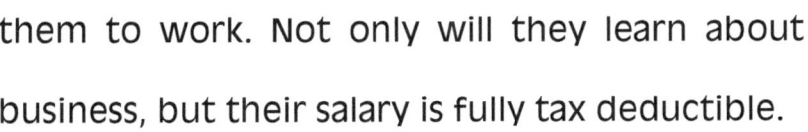 ance, you hire your kids and put them to work. Not only will they learn about business, but their salary is fully tax deductible.

Moving Expenses. Do you have to move? Have your company pay for it. Whether it is across town or across the country, your company can pay for an executive move and it is deductible.

♦♦♦♦

GC: These are not GRAY area deductions. These are mainstream deductions that all business owners are eligible to take.

At the beginning, I asked you if you were losing money? The answer is YES: every single day.

By not taking steps to make yourself eligible for these deductions, you are literally throwing money away.

**So what are you waiting for?
Start a business from your home!**

AGELATIONS REAL WORLD EXAMPLE

Sally has recently been introduced to a network marketing opportunity that sells nutritional supplements. To get started, she figures her startup costs to be around $1690.00. Sally is unsure whether or not she will be able to recoup these expenses.

She presently works a full time job, earning $40,000 per year and pays approximately $10,000 per year in taxes.

Assuming she doesn't sell a lot in her new endeavor but makes a conscientious effort to build her business, is it still worthwhile for her to at least give the opportunity a try? Let's take a look:

1. First Year Expenses:

In Sally's business, she must purchase an initial business kit ($250) and continue buying supplements for marketing and promotion purposes on a monthly basis ($120 per mo.)

$ 250.00	Initial enrollment cost.
+ 1440.00	Additional supplements for year one.

$ 1690.00	**Total cost for the first year.**

 This is the total anticipated cost of running her network marketing business during the first year of operation.

The IRS has ruled that up to $5000 of direct startup costs can be deducted in the year they are accrued. In other words, year one.

So, to start recouping her investment, we take the initial startup purchase and calculate the actual savings by multiplying it by her tax bracket. Most of us are in the 25% bracket, so for simplicity let's use this percentage.

$250.00 x .25 = $62.50

$1690 – $62.50 = $1627.50 remaining.

2. Mileage

Sally drove 8920 deductible miles during her first year of business. Using the 2008 deduction of $0.585 cents per mile, this equates to the following:

8920 miles x $0.585 cents per mile = $5218.20 for the year.

Calculate the actual tax savings:

$5218.20 x .25 (tax rate) = $ 1304.55

So, to our ongoing tally:

$1627.50 (total remaining expenses) – $1304.55 = $322.95 in expenses left to recoup.

3. Marketing

The direct costs of conducting business are 100% deductible. If we go back to our year 1 startup costs, we need to deduct our marketing expense. In other words, the monthly supplement purchases.

$1440 x .25 (tax rate) = $360.00

After our deduction for mileage, only $322.95 worth of expenses remained.

$322.95 – $360.00 = $(37.05)

Thus, $37.05 has been added to her federal tax **REFUND** without getting to the MAJOR deduction possibilities or without making a single sale!

4. Meals and Entertainment

Remember, you can deduct 50% of your business related meals and entertainment expenses. Sally had $756 of such meal-related expenses during her first year in business.

So: we can take 50%,

$756 x .5 = $378

Total tax savings: $378 x .25 (tax rate) = **$94.50**

Her tax **REFUND** has now increased:
$37.05 + 94.50 = **$131.55.**

During that same year, Sally took a vacation to Las Vegas, where her network marketing company was also having a training class that same time. She combined her trip with the training, thus making it deductible.

For our example, we will assume she purchased a $2000 vacation package.

So, $2000 x .5 (we can only deduct 50%) = $1000

Tax savings:

$1000 x .25 = **$250**

Her **refund** continues to grow: $131.55 + $250.00 = **$381.55** AND COUNTING.

5. Home-based business Office

For our example, Sally utilizes 12% of her home as her 'home office' where she runs her business. She had $1800 in total utility costs per year.

So, $1800 x .12 = $216.00

Tax savings:

$216 x .25 = **$54.00**

So, Sally's **refund** is now $381.55 + 54.00 = $**435.55**

Keep in mind that this will also increase her state refund as well (if state tax is applicable). All business expenses are deducted from your adjusted gross income and this is used to compute your state tax.

This example demonstrates how Sally was able to increase her tax refund by an amount of $435.55. This could easily increase as she goes through more of the legal deductions due to the large number of deductions available. This could literally amount to thousands of dollars. It really depends on the individual's circumstances.

If it is so easy, why doesn't everyone take advantage of it? We do not have a good answer. Either they lack motivation, don't want to mess with the record keeping, or just don't know that these rules exist for their benefit.

Will you let these obstacles stop you?

IV. Real Estate

"The less I do, the more I make."
– Ron LeGrand

The Law of Serendipity

GV: I can still remember the first rental house I bought back in 2004. It was a little 2-bedroom garage apartment in my home town of Clarksburg, a small West Virginia town where I grew up. My reasons for getting into real estate might surprise you.

I was actually in a really good job. My wife Carla and I really didn't need the money nor had any thoughts of real estate investing during our first three years of marriage (we were married in 2001). It actually started differently than what you would expect...

When I met Carla, she was just finishing her Master of Science degree in Chemistry at Marshall University in Huntington, WV. When we got married, she moved to Clarksburg, as I was already in a steady, full-time career there. Although she pursued many openings, she was unable to find employment in the science field. There just weren't that many scientific jobs in our community.

She did land some part time work at a local university teaching Organic Chemistry and took another part time job in the Pharmacy at our local Wal-Mart.

Within 8 months, she worked her way up to store manager and was transferred to

Morgantown, West Virginia, about 30 miles away.

It didn't take her long to realize that being a store manager was a far cry from being a Chemist. She worked gruelingly long hours and I never saw her, even on her days off.

One day, we analyzed her $30K a year salary against her hours and realized that she was actually earning less than minimum wage! It was time for a change.

Around that time, I was reading two books: *Rich Dad Poor Dad* by Robert Kiyosaki and *How To Make Big Money In Real Estate* by Tyler Hicks. What I derived from this was that Carla and I could buy apartments and make more *passively* than her working full-time in her job doing something she hated.

That year, we purchased the aforementioned garage apartment and a 4 bedroom house, also in Clarksburg. I started this chapter with the subheading: The Law of Serendipity. These days, there is a big to do about The Law of Attraction, as evidenced by the success of the widely popular *The Secret* and many other books dealing with that subject.

However, I would like to talk to you about The Law of Serendipity. The Law of Serendipity basically states that while you are pursuing one goal another opportunity will present itself to you that is far greater than the one you are pursuing.

To put it a different way: while you are knocking on Door A, a bigger and better opportunity will reveal itself to you behind Door B, however you would not be aware of its existence had you not been in the hallway knocking on Door A.

The Law of Serendipity is also closely linked to the Law of Multiplicity: the universe will give you more if you are a good steward with what you have.

After we bought the second investment house, Carla and I decided to attend a real estate wealth building expo sponsored by The Learning Annex in New York. There, we were exposed to ideas by real estate greats like Ron LeGrand, Donald Trump, Robert Kiyosaki, Robert Shemin, and many others.

There was one 'guru' in particular who was giving a speech during the lunch break. Carla and I were hungry and we definitely could have skipped it, however at my urging we went to listen what this gentleman had to say. On the stage was Canadian Entrepreneur and wealth coach T. Harv Eker.

This man delved into the psychology of wealth and gave all who attended the lunch lecture tickets to his *Millionaire Mind Intensive*, a three day boot camp on getting your head wrapped around what it means to think like a millionaire.

Little did I know, The Law of Serendipity was at work. By just *being there,* Carla and I created a new opportunity for ourselves. As I look back, I can see a unique pattern of events: we read quality publications, bought our first investment properties, attended seminars, skipped lunch and got financial training.

Shortly thereafter, Carla and I went to Tampa, FL, where we learned about real estate investing techniques from another person who was there at The Learning Annex: Ron LeGrand.

I've heard it from several people that Mr. LeGrand has made more millionaires in America than anyone else. I am inclined to believe it as Carla and I are living examples of principle put into practice.

A unique paradigm began to develop: up till 2004, Carla our *lifetime* net worth was $120K, including our residence. By 2005, we doubled this; by 2006, it was $350K, by 2007, it was half a million, by 2008, it was $1.2 million, and by 2009 this is set to double; all from real estate.

Now I realize that some people reading this book may have houses worth more than the highest figure I mentioned above. I would like to point out however, that Carla and I both came from very humble beginnings.

Carla is an immigrant from Cochabamba, Boliva. I grew up in West Virginia, one of the poorest states in the United States. The average household income in WV is $28K per year, and that is a two income-producing family! Growing up, our family made due with less than $20K per year. In comparison, the national average is just under $50K per year.

As we are products of our environment, it is nothing short of a miracle that we were able to break tradition and become so much more, so quickly. We raised our financial baseline through training and practice. The Laws of Serendipity and Multiplicity working hand in hand enabled us to go further than we ever imagined.

Why Invest in Real Estate?

There are many reasons why to invest in real estate. For starters, people always need a place to live; it's one of the three necessities of life (food, clothing, and *shelter*). It is also all around us – you can't go anywhere without being near real estate.

However, if I were to give three top reasons why, they would be leverage, depreciation, and appreciation.

Leverage is the ability to buy something with borrowed money and use the cash flow from this purchase to pay off its debt.

Depreciation is being able to write off the value of the real estate asset over time for tax purposes in order to defer (not avoid) paying tax on the profits.

Appreciation is the equity that is created in the real estate when the debt is paid off and/or the market takes an upswing in the value of the area in which the real estate is located.

Pitfalls of Real Estate Investing

I can't really stress enough how important a good education is when it comes to real estate investing. My training with Ron LeGrand has taught me much; plus the School of Hard Knocks has taught me a great deal as well. As I teach you some of what I learned along the way, just remember that no book alone should be your stand-alone guide to getting rich in this field.

Life is an ongoing education and you should always invest in yourself: be it our products, a LeGrand seminar, something from The Learning Annex - **just get out there and get your training.**

Remember this Dear Reader: if you think education is expensive, wait until you see the cost of ignorance! One way or another, you'll pay for a seminar.

So, let's begin by looking at what NOT to do when investing in Real Estate:

1. **Don't write big check; don't lose big check.** I learned this from Ron. Be very cautious of large down payments. Unless you are doing something in the commercial real estate field, there are

ways to buy a house without the large down payment. This is typically done in transactions that *don't* involve a Realtor.

2. **Avoid using your credit whenever possible.** There are many real estate gurus out there that teach you how to buy a house with 'no money down.' They profess that you get the down payment from a credit card and finance the mortgage with a traditional bank loan. Your credit is very valuable; protect it at all costs! Once you learn how to buy real estate like the rich do, you will discover that houses are really a dime a dozen and

there are so many out there that you can buy with either seller financing or taking over a note subject to its original terms and conditions (more on that later) that you would be crazy to put your own credit at risk.

3. **Avoid doing closings yourself.** Once you learn how to buy houses on the fly, you will be tempted to use a standard purchase and sales agreement to close the deal yourself and avoid attorney/title agent fees. Reader, don't give in to this temptation. Having an official closing with an agent who understands your mode of operation will save you much grief in the long

run; especially if the other party forgets the agreement once their circumstances have changed.

4. **Avoid making false claims to get a deal done.** Only a very small percentage of real estate investors out there are unscrupulous. However, it only takes a few of these individuals to get us placed in a bad light and Attorney Generals are ever to eager to pass laws to stifle our efforts in making a legitimate living in this field. Jail time or a bad reputation is not worth any house deal.

5. Avoid seller financing with friends and family. This goes both ways; whether you are buying or selling. I don't think I need to get into the complexities of what can happen when you do business with friends and relatives, especially when long or short term financing is involved. Don't go there unless it's an all cash deal.

Winning Real Estate Strategies

Real Estate investing is a vast topic. There are countless books and seminars on the subject. What I am going to do is take some of the most effective methods that have worked for me, introduce them to you, and let you decide for yourself which of these make sense for you, based on your own specific circumstances in life.

I would recommend you take what you like, leave what you don't, and go get educated further on that which interests you. We have included a references website at the end of this book that will help assist you in this regard. By no means is this an all-inclusive list, but it will definitely get you started in learning the subject.

Ugly Houses

As the name implies, this is the art of buying an ugly, fixer-upper house in need of repair and selling it. Most of the time these deals are all cash transactions, as typically a bank will not touch a house if it has substantial issues that need to be addressed.

Wholesaling. If you buy the house and sell it to a rehabber, this is called "wholesaleing." Optionally, you can buy the house, fix it yourself, and sell it for full market value and this is called "retailing."

Many people start their Real Estate investing careers in ugly houses. It can be challenging dealing with the low-end junkers, so be warned up front.

A skilled wholesaler can line up a subject property and have the buyer in queue so that at closing, they can buy the house and simultaneously sell the house to the end buyer (the rehabber.) This is known as a "simultaneous closing."

If you don't have much money, wholesaleing houses may be a good way to get started. The typical deal generates between $5,000 - $10,000 profit and if you did one a month, it can give you some starter capital to venture into new areas.

Determining the ARV and MAO. One of the most important skills you will need when dealing with junkers is knowing how to determine the After Repair Value (or ARV) of a property and the Maximum Allowable Offer (or MAO) you are willing to pay for it. Keep this formula in mind:

[(ARV * .65) – repairs] - $5000.00 = MAO

In the above formula, you get the ARV by looking at comparables. These are houses in the **same neighborhood** that have the same general features (number of bedrooms, number of bathrooms, number of stories, etc.) that have sold recently.

The .65 represents 65% of the worth of the finished product. The repairs are how much you estimate it will cost you to fix the subject property. And, the last $5000.00 is for the "X" factor of unknown expenses or, it can be considered your profit if you are wholesaling the deal to a rehabber.

Pretty Houses

Pretty houses need very little work, except maybe some minor cleaning and cosmetics. Most are expensive enough that you will need some type of financing arrangement in order to buy them.

How you buy a pretty house is up to you, but let me give you some secrets to keeping this business doable, especially if you don't have much money:

Look for motivated sellers. Although this can be true for any Real Estate investing, it is especially true for the Pretty House buyer.

You most likely will not find the motivated sellers via Realtors, as they are trying to sell the house for maximum retail price. No, these individuals will need to be approached via non-traditional means (i.e., direct mail, calling the owner of a vacant house, searching expired listings, probate, etc.).

Consider a "Subject To" transaction. A lot of people are trying to get out from under their mortgage. Many are motivated to the point that they are willing to deed you their house so that you will cover that mortgage payment while they move on with their lives.

Who are these people, you might ask? Some people have lost their jobs, been transferred, gone through a divorce, inherited the property and so on and so forth. The last thing they need is another payment to make. If you can offer to make the payment for them, a mutually-beneficial agreement may be arranged.

In a "Subject To" transaction, the Buyer (you) will take title to the property with the Seller's original mortgage intact. Only the title (deed) transfers from the Seller to You. The mortgage (deed of trust) is a lien that will stay on the property.

The loan does not get assumed by you. Let me repeat this in a different way: you are not going to go down to the bank and get a new mortgage to buy the Pretty House.

Your goal in a "Subject To" deal is to put a tenant or new home buyer in the house and make the mortgage payments with the new tenant's rent. You secure the house without using your credit and in many cases, little or no down payment.

Buying a house this way gives you unlimited purchasing capabilities, as you are not limited to the amount you can personally borrow since the mortgage is not in your name.

I am sure that many of you are screaming right now saying to yourself, "That's not right! No one will sell me their house this way! Plus, doesn't the bank have a 'Due on Sale' clause that prevents a deed from transferring to a new owner without it first being paid off?"

This concept may be very hard to grasp for many of you, but the truth is, banks really don't want houses back. They would much rather see a performing asset then a non-performing one. Many of the houses offered by motivated sellers are on the verge of foreclosure. The banks are delighted to see the payment streams re-established.

Now, are you going to run down to the bank and get their permission to perform a "Subject To" transaction? No.

What you are going to do is have the seller sign a "CYA" (or "Cover Your **Ass**ets") letter in front of an attorney or closing agent that acknowledges the loan will remain in their (the

Seller's) name until paid off **and** that the loan contains a "Due on Sale" Clause.

The Due on Sale Clause means that the bank, at their sole discretion, **may** choose to call the loan due if they discover that title has transferred. In other words, the loan would be payable **in full** immediately.

If this happens, you (the Buyer) are not obligated to pay off the loan and should that occur, the house may be foreclosed by the bank. The Seller also acknowledges that he/she will hold you harmless should such an action be taken by the bank.

Every mortgage made after 1984 has this language in it. I have purchased several houses

Subject To in my time and have never had the bank call the loan due.

Before I move to my next subject in real estate investing, I want to make a point here on ethics: if you do tell a Seller that you are going to make his/her payments, then be sure to do it. Don't say one thing and do another. It is a crime to take over a house Subject To, then not make the payments, while at the same time, putting a renter or new buyer into the house. This is known as equity skimming and will get you jail time.

Also, be aware that although purchasing a house Subject To is not illegal, you should familiarize yourself with local laws regarding the matter. Remember, you are not a foreclosure consultant when dealing with a Seller and you cannot claim that you buying their house will keep them out of foreclosure.

Also, some states mandate that you must have a Realtor's license prior to engaging in Subject To transactions. Just know what the rules are in your state.

Consider Seller Financing. Many houses, especially free and clear ones, can be bought with seller financing. This is preferred if you can get the deed to the house. A seller financed house is not usually reported on your personal credit report as a bank financed house would be, so this is always a plus.

Remember, the more houses you can buy that are not on your personal credit, the longer you can afford to stay in the game and buy even more houses!

Commercial Real Estate

Commercial Real Estate is a very big topic and probably too big to cover in this book. I will, however go over a few areas that I would (and do) invest in, along with my #1 favorite way to purchase commercial properties.

When you deal with commercial real estate, be aware that you are in a much more expensive game than the residential market.

Consequently, you will have skin in the game. You must do due diligence when dealing in commercial. Shortcuts that you might get by with in residential will not fly on these larger projects. These deals also take a lot longer on average and you need to have a good head at the get go to endure the marathon that awaits you.

That being said, commercial real estate is also where you can earn the big bucks. Ron LeGrand had a funny saying that goes something like this: "The more dollars you wallow in, the more that stick to you."

Multiplex Apartments. After buying my first two rental houses (both single-family homes), my wife and I decided to buy our first multiple unit apartment building, or multiplex for short. I've bought several others since then and here's what I've learned:

Multiplexes are good for new investors who want cash flow. They also seem to be easier to sell than other types of commercial properties such as undeveloped land, industrial warehouses, shopping centers, etc.

If you were to purchase a multiplex, it is conceivable that you could make a profit when you sell it; especially if you keep it fixed up and increase the rents over time. This is a type of property that many real estate investors want and the time on the market would be less than say, a vacant factory. I also think your overall risks would be less too.

Self Storage Units. If I had to pick my favorite type of real estate investment, it would be the self storage facility. These businesses, if managed correctly, are cash cows with low overhead and easier to manage when compared to apartments.

Here's why: when customers don't pay, we lock up their stuff. If they still don't pay, their names are published in the local newspaper. If they remain in default, we auction the stuff and keep the money. That's my kind of management! Also, it's much easier to remove a non-payer from a self storage unit, than when they are living in a house or apartment.

The drawbacks of self storage investing are that you have many transactions to deal with each month. Consequently, you need to be at the top of your game to keep up with the administration.

If you have 300 storage units, for example, that means that you have 300 accounts to manage, 300 monthly invoices to mail out, 300 payments to process, etc. That on top of answering phone calls, making reservations, and following up on the non-payers.

The key to maintaining your sanity in self storage is to have systems in place to make some of the work easier. Consider having an employee or independent company handle the phones.

Have a property manager for the onsite day-to-day activities. Use online accounting systems specifically written for the self storage industry to keep track of tenants and reservations. And, accept credit cards and electronic checks to capture as many customers as possible.

Structuring a Commercial Deal

Understanding CAP Rate. Before you begin structuring your deal, it may be best that you determine the property's capitalization rate (or cap for short). This is often misunderstood by investors, so I will try to break it down in simple terms here.

Cap rate is determined by dividing the **net operating income (NOI)** of the sale comparables by the sale price. Let's say you are investing in a $300,000.00 self storage facility. If the NOI of similar facilities in the area is $30,000.00 annually, the subject property would have a cap 10:

$300,000 / $30,000 = 10

If the comps were $25K annually, the cap rate would be 12 and conversely, if the comps were $35K annually, the cap rate would be 8.5.

WHEN DETERMINING CAP RATE REMEMBER:

THE LOWER THE NUMBER THE BETTER THE INVESTMENT.

Of course, the cap rate's accuracy depends on the accuracy of several factors: the buyer's objectives, appraisal(s), market information, and how accurate the income figures are, especially when analyzing the NOI.

The Rule of 10. Many people get cap rate confused with another way of looking at a deal that I call "The Rule of 10." How this works is you take your NOI multiply it by 10 and see how that value relates to the purchase price of the property you are wishing to buy.

I take this one step further and look at it this way. If I stuck the same amount of money in the bank, drawing 10% interest which is the better investment? It's kind of a high-level litmus test to see how realistic the deal is. Usually you want your investment property to get no less than an 8% return, 10% is better, and so forth and so on.

How to Determine NOI When You Don't Know?

Never purchase a commercial property without first doing due diligence. However, you may want to see if the investment is worth pursing by taking a SWAG at the numbers. (SWAG, by the way, is an acronym for "Scientific Wild Ass Guess").

If everything was rented at its current market rates, that would be the Gross Operating Income (GOI). Take the annual GOI and multiply it by .65 to get 65% of the GOI. I affectionately call this the SWAG NOI.

The property's mortgage payment and your salary need to come from the SWAG NOI.

Ask yourself, "Does the property cash flow with these figures?" If the answer is, "Yes," then you are ready to take the next step, make an offer and begin your due diligence.

If no, consider making an offer that is more in line with profitability than what the seller's inflated aspirations are.

Seller Subordination – My #1 favorite way to purchase commercial properties.

More often than not, commercial properties take a long time to sell. They are much more expensive than single-family houses and consequently, more is involved in getting them financed.

Donald Trump has mentioned that one way of knowing if purchasing an existing business is good or not is whether the seller will finance part of it. This principle can be applied here. If a seller is motivated and trusts their property will cash flow through term, they may be willing to seller finance all or part of the deal.

Each of my self storage facilities had some degree of seller financing or I would not have bought them. To help illustrate my point, I will describe my Dartmoor Storage deal below.

The seller wanted $189,900 for his 40-unit storage facility in Dartmoor, WV. The GOI on the property was $19,200, making the SWAG NOI $12,480. Based on the NOI, it was clear that the property would not cash flow for its current price or an outright sale.

We negotiated a sales price of $165,000. However, it was not an all-cash deal because that payment was still too high. The seller took $110,000 cash and *subordinated* to a second position mortgage for his remaining $55,000.

This second mortgage had no payments for the first five years!

Because the market value of the property was $192,000, the bank had no problem lending up to $125,000.00 and holding a first-position mortgage on the property. The seller's remaining $55,000 was in second position.

Consequently, I was able to buy the storage business with **no money down** and walk away with $15,000 at closing! This is an example of seller subordinated financing.

Tax Lien/Deed Investing. The last category of real estate investing that I want to talk about in this book is probably the safest. It's government-backed and has been somewhat of a secret of wealthy real estate investors as this category gets very little attention.

We live in turbulent economic times and for this very reason, many people have found themselves incapable (or at least reluctant) to pay their real estate property taxes.

Municipalities around the country have made collecting these taxes a top priority. Without the revenues these taxes provide, core government services such as police protection, fire, schools, etc., could be jeopardized.

In an effort to insure they are able to collect these taxes, the county attaches a lien to the tax delinquent properties. I often think of this as the "master lien" on a property. It is always there, in first position, but never triggered until you don't pay your taxes.

The county auctions these liens to investors at a public tax sale. Afterwards, a tax lien certificate is awarded to the investor with the winning bid. These sales occur at different times throughout the year based on municipality and some require you be in person and others are on the Internet.

If you are a winning bidder of a tax lien certificate, several benefits occur: the county gets their money, the homeowner now has more time to pay their delinquent property taxes, and you, the investor, now have a real estate-backed, interest-bearing instrument. What a great way to invest your money!

Understand that in this arena of real estate investing, you have virtually no market risk. Unlike the ups and downs of security based trading (stocks, bonds, etc.) the interest that a tax lien certificate pays is fixed by state law. So, if that low-yielding bank certificate of deposit is not your fancy, consider placing these funds in a tax lien certificate instead.

If you are not fond of riskier types of investments like stocks, then tax liens and tax deeds are ideal. In relation to tax lien certificates, the county government will collect the back taxes plus interest from the delinquent property holder, and then send you a check for your principal (the amount you paid for the certificate) plus interest.

This is quite a nice process and don't forget: at no time are you dealing with the property owner!

So, "Are the interest rates good," you might ask? In Florida rates are fixed at 18% APR! In Arizona its 16%, in West Virginia it's 12% just to name a few.

I know you are probably thinking, "Okay, these rates are nice, but what if the property owner doesn't pay his taxes at all?" If that happens, my friend, you have hit the jackpot! After a certain period of time (it varies from state to state), you can seek the property as collateral. Basically, you own the property for its taxes!

The nice thing is, you don't have to have a lot of money to invest in tax lien certificates. These are sold from anywhere from a few dollars to millions. There's something for everyone. You ought to give it a try.

My wife and I once purchased two building lots valued at over $30,000.00 for only the $200.00 of back taxes that were owed! These lots were used as collateral to build our storage facility, VIP Storage, in Fairmont, WV.

Okay, now that I mentioned tax lien certificates, I want to talk about the other possibility: a tax deed. Some states/counties prefer this method to collect their delinquent property taxes. As this varies from state to state, you'll need to check your target area to see what process your jurisdiction falls under.

In a tax deed process, the government auctions the property to the winning bidder to get their back taxes.

In these circumstances two things can happen:

1. The county auctions the property and the sale is final. The winning bidder receives a deed to the property.

2. The county auctions the property, but the deed is restricted by a waiting period or redemption period in which the delinquent property owner can pay the tax and penalty, and get to keep the property.

Texas is such a state, but fret not, as you would earn 25% ***every six months*** if you buy a tax deed in Texas and it does end up getting redeemed!

*If you like the idea of tax lien/tax deed investing or other areas of real estate, consider purchasing our **Agelations Home Study Course** and subscribing to **The Profiteer**, our monthly newsletter.*

See the Resources section in the back of this book for more information.

V. Information Marketing

*"As a rule, he or she who has the most information
will have the greatest success in life."*
— Herbert Simon

The Most Profitable Business You'll Ever Have

GV: Let me start this chapter by stating that I do not support "Get Rich Quick" schemes and think that if it is too good to be true, it probably is. However, if you want to get rich quicker than other wealth producing models described in this book, Information Marketing is something you will want to consider.

We live in an Information Age. In prior generations, people depended upon industry to make the world work; today it is information.

I say this may be the most profitable business model here because information is everywhere you look and very inexpensive to assimilate. As long as a person knows their audience (market), then an information product can be produced for that audience. This does not require talent, only knowledge of the market.

It also does not require a great deal of money. With the use of the Internet, on-demand publishing, and electronic distribution, these information products can be created for virtually nothing and sold for thousands of dollars. It is the only model that has virtually no startup costs.

So, where do you begin if you want to pursue this very profitable field?

Becoming A Polymath

I originally thought about titling this section "Becoming A Renaissance Man," but realized that I might offend the female readers who are just as talented as us guys. Not only that, it might have brought confusion thinking that I was talking about painters from a bygone era. So, I decided to go with "Becoming a Polymath," an awkward heading, I admit, but it will make sense as we go along.

Back when I was in high school, music was a big hobby of mine. Not only did I sing, but I also played the guitar and wrote several songs. Early on, I pitched my works to various musicians and some were even recorded. Later, I recorded my own music and released a couple albums as an Independent (or "Indie") Artist under my self-created "VINCE" record label. Little did I know that I was taking part in Information Marketing at the time.

In those early years, I was able to successfully get my songs distributed on websites and on radio, and eventually got them onto media outlets such as Apple's iTunes service. As a result of what I did *in high school*, I receive royalties even to this day on these early songs.

After graduating from college, I wrote an autobiography titled: *The Winner, The Loser: The Story of My Life At 21.*

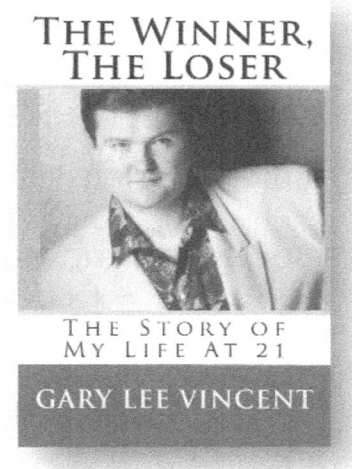

The Winner, The Loser contained a series of life philosophies and my outlook on life *before* I made it big. It's worth picking up a copy to see some of my earlier thoughts about life and how I applied it to get to where I'm at today. Why do I mention it here? *The Winner, The Loser* is **another** type of information product to compliment the music CDs that my fans enjoyed.

So, what is a Polymath? This is actually taken from the Greek word "polymathēs" meaning, having learned much. It refers to a person that is knowledgeable in many different subjects.

As *Agelations* deals with many topics, it is polymath in nature. It is the belief of George and me both that you need to be a polymath and learn as much as you can on many different subjects. That was why this book was created and why we developed Agelity, Inc. of Nevada and the **www.HomeBizMarketeer.com** websites to assist you in the pursuit of knowledge.

Why? The more knowledge that you have the more effective you can be, whether in life or in the products you create. All you have to do is identify your market (target audience) and then create an information product that caters to that audience.

Be A Specialist. It is important for you to be as specialized as possible because if customers can identify that **your** item teaches them from A to Z about the subject matter they are interested in, *in a specialized way,* then they will buy from you!

What do I mean by 'in a specialized way'? Let's say you created a cookbook for making different types of hamburgers. The specialist information marketer would customize the title of the book: *John Doe's Ultra Awesome Hamburger Cookbook: 27 Amazing Recipes That*

Will Rock Your Grill!

This sounds a whole lot better than the non-specialized title: *Cookbook for Hamburgers.* Based on the title, which would you buy?

Deliver The Goods. Your information has to be good or your business will ultimately fail. Even if you can get a sale of a bad product, you will have tarnished your reputation for future sales from that customer.

However, if you deliver a good information product, you will have a satisfied customer who will much more likely be buying many more future items from you. Don't overlook this! Garbage will ruin your information marketing business. Deliver good quality information and be ready for repeat business.

Also *deliver the goods* literally. In other words, your information product must be able to be delivered in a timely manner. Don't take orders and not fill them.

That only makes common sense, but too often, an information marketer will be manufacturing the products from home and get too busy to fill the orders. Don't let this happen to you!

Try to use services (such as automatic downloads for eBook purchases) whenever possible to get your information product out the door as the orders come in.

Isolate Your Customers. A customer is worth *a lot* of money. Their value lies not only in the one-time sale, but in a lifetime of business for you. Thus, it is important to separate your customers from the rest of the marketplace.

It is also important to realize that you cannot capture the entire market, thus you need to find a target audience in which to promote your product. This is typically done through lead generation.

In lead generation, you are not trying to sell your products but find customers in your target market to advertise to on a steady, ongoing basis. This is especially true in information marketing.

Your initial media should not sell the customer an item but rather pitch to the market as a whole, a free or near free item that will bring qualified leads to you. Once you have leads for the 'free' item, that item will then serve as a gateway to promote your information product.

You will also keep the lead for future promotional campaigns, because since they responded before, you have a foresight into knowing that these are select customers in your market who are interested in your items and much more likely to buy from you. In other words, they are *qualified.*

Other ways to generate leads are through print advertising, internet advertising, direct mail, creating articles, and speaking engagements just to name a few. Keep in mind that the most successful information marketers use more than one lead generation method, so consider using several different approaches to find the one that works best for your particular product.

What To Create

You are smarter than you think. I believe that everybody has unique, God-given gifts. Every one of us knows something that may be of interest to someone. If you don't, you may want to check your pulse!

In a nutshell, Information Marketing is being able to take some subject matter in which you have knowledge and create a product that others can buy and learn from.

You don't need to have musical talent as I described in my high school example, although that is one type of information product. You may have a hobby that you can write about, or maybe you yourself are interested in learning about something and took the time to research that topic. You can put your research to use to make something that others can benefit from.

But What If You Don't Know How To Write?

I have a friend who is a retired State Police dispatcher who worked in his job for over 20 years. There have been countless times he told me of different stories that happened on the job that were intriguing and genuinely interesting. He was not a writer, but I told him to take a recorder and just talk about the stories as if he were telling it to me conversationally. Once recorded, these stories could be transcribed and a book about *The Life and Times of a State Police Dispatcher* could be published. Best part, the stories were so interesting that not only would the book be great, I could see how several screen plays could be adopted, all from his experiences!

But What If You're Not Very Interesting?

If you really don't want to write or record you own unique product, you can always license someone else's work and resell it. Think about your own interests and look at your own personal library. What have you bought or read lately? Could you create a book review on the Internet with a link to someplace like amazon.com and derive an affiliate commission for your reviews? Just some food for thought.

Information Marketing Examples

Information exists in many forms. Below are just some of the formats you can use to market your information:

Printed items. These include books, reports, manuals, newsletters, home study courses, posters, calendars, cards, and academic items (like tests and forms).

Multimedia items. These are audio / visual in nature and include audio tapes and CDs and DVDs. Some examples of information products on tape are live recordings of seminars or public speeches, trainings, radio shows, how-to / instructional programs, interviews, and interactive do-it-yourself programs.

eProducts. These are items that can be delivered digitally through the Internet. Examples include eBooks, membership sites, software, streaming audio or video, digital photographs, assembly or instruction manuals; basically anything that can be downloaded.

Be A Public Speaker

Just as having an information product can make you an expert (or at least a specialist) in a particular field, becoming a speaker can allow you to earn multiple times more money for your information products.

An event speaker can earn over $100,000 in a weekend! I have personally witnessed the phenomena. I have been to events such as The Learning Annex's Real Estate Expo where I saw thousands of people gathered to hear an expert talk about a given subject.

After the speech was over, they offered their information product for several hundred to several thousand dollars and I witnessed people by the droves lining up at the back of the room to buy the products!

My friend Ron LeGrand is a good example of this: he sells a boot camp for $2995.00 on real estate investing. I have been to events where he pitched this program and over a hundred people bought it (I was one of them).

Reader get your head around this: that was over $300,000 earned in one event, not to mention Ron now has a customer base and multiple follow-up products to offer to his students.

Real Estate Guru Ron LeGrand and Gary Vincent on a
Financial Freedom Network Cruise

Now, I know that public speaking puts the
fear of God in most people and that many
reading this would prefer not to do it, however
if you really want to accelerate your
information marketing business, public
speaking is the way to go!

Remember, you don't have to wait until
you're up in front of people giving a speech

before you sell your information product in the back of the room. You can use direct mail, industry publications, and the Internet to build the fan base and start selling the products even before you step foot on stage.

Develop Your Package

Your information product should not be one isolated item. Many novice information marketers drop the ball here. When you address a market, have in mind a set of items. In other words, back end information products.

Here is an example of the item, its cost, and the follow-up items:

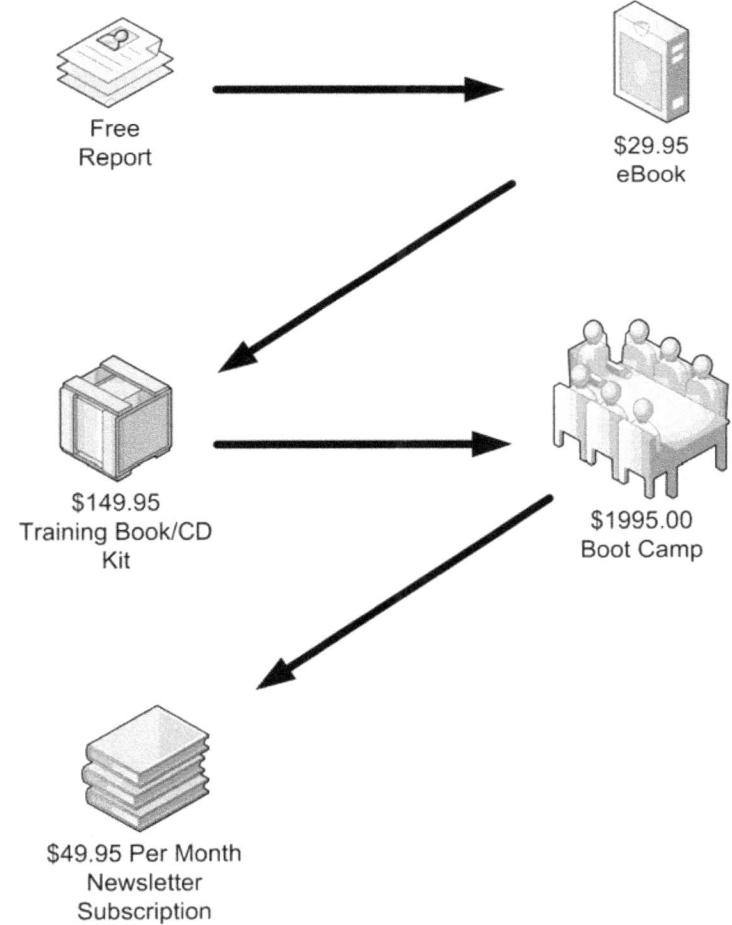

Free
Report

$29.95
eBook

$149.95
Training Book/CD
Kit

$1995.00
Boot Camp

$49.95 Per Month
Newsletter
Subscription

You get the picture. Be the expert and have follow-up products in your field of expertise.

Can you see yourself getting wealthy with Information Marketing? If so, purchase our **Agelations Home Study Course** *and subscribe to* **The Profiteer**, *our monthly newsletter, for many great ways to help you succeed in this realm.*

See the Resources section in the back of this book for more information.

VI. Network Marketing Defined

"We can have more than we've got because
we can become more than we are."
– Jim Rohn

GC: Network marketing began in the late 1950's and has become a mega success with in excess of $100 billion in annual sales. I have been asked on numerous occasions to describe the exact meaning of "network marketing".

I believe that the simplest answer is that network marketing is the use of an individual's personal network (friends, family, and associates) to create a framework for the sale of a given commodity, be it a service or a product.

This in turn leads to an ever expanding group of individuals pursuing a similar business goal as each of your networking associates promotes the commodity to their own "network" thus creating a wealth generating mechanism for all.

◆◆◆◆

Time Independence

GV: Network marketing, or multi-level marketing (MLM) as some people call it, is a way to leverage the time and efforts of others to accomplish more than what you alone can achieve.

Consider this example: when you go to bed at night, does the interest on your home mortgage stop accruing when you go to sleep? The answer is no.

Remember in Chapter 2, I described the limitations to trading hours for dollars and that you only have a finite number that you personally can contribute? With network marketing, you combine your time with others to create an infinite pool of hours, limited only to the size of your organization.

Think of it this way, if 100 people contributed only 4 hours per week to the business, you would have a 400 hour work week! This is what I mean by "leverage." Even if you worked a 'double' full-time shift, 80 hours is still not even 25% of what the network can do working only 5% of those hours!

Get your head around this: you can go much further with a network than what you can achieve solely on your own.

◆◆◆◆

Are you a full time spender and a part time earner?

GC: When you think about your current job, ask yourself this question: Is the work that you do completely dependent on your ability to generate income or do you have others working for you that help leverage your time?

To put it another way, "If you step away from your business do you stop generating income?" If this is indeed the case, then you are a FULL TIME SPENDER and a PART TIME EARNER.

What do I mean by this statement?

As Gary mentioned above, most of us have recurring debts each month: mortgage, utilities, car payments, credit cards, etc. The interest that you incur for borrowing this money accrues every hour of every day.

When you are self-employed (non-MLM speaking) or work in a traditional job, your income is completely based on the number of hours that you can work. Hence you are a FULL TIME SPENDER and a PART TIME EARNER. This is the main reason that I am a strong proponent of network marketing.

In network marketing, you create a team of networked dealers and customers that both buy and sell a given product or service. You use the coordinated efforts of many individuals to generate income. Once in place, you will be a FULL TIME EARNER and PART TIME SPENDER.

◆◆◆◆

How Does It Work?
(Understanding the "Comp" Plan)

GV: There have been entire books and presentations dedicated to explaining how network marketing works. Many in the industry refer to this as the compensation plan (or comp plan for short.) To be honest, this can be very confusing and scares away many who don't understand it.

Comp plans vary from company to company. Some operate in a lateral structure, some have break away structures, and others have binaries. There are several out there.

Because the goal of *Agelations* is to give you fundamental strategies that will assist you regardless of how your company's comp plan works, we have specifically chosen not to go into a vast explanation of the different types of comp plans out there.

It is, however, a good learning tool, so that I will describe a very basic example of one of the more commonly used models to help you gain an understanding as to how network marketing works, how products are sold, and how money is made.

Let me start by saying that network marketing is **not** a pyramid scheme to launder money from friends and family. Those are illegal and we will discuss how to recognize them later in this book.

In network marketing, the customer and the network are one in the same. Rather than have a traditional store front, a sponsor introduces a new customer to the product or services of his/her company and that person in turn, introduces the products or services to someone else.

This 'word of mouth' advertising creates an ever-expanding consumer base. Much like referring someone to a good restaurant or movie, you refer the person to the network marketing company's product or service. The primary difference here is that you get paid for this referral.

As your customer base grows, you get a monthly income on the volume of merchandise they purchase. As the number of customers in your group expands, so does your income.

The person who introduces you to the opportunity is known as the Sponsor. He/she is considered to be part of your "Upline."

The Sponsor will earn a commission on any products that you purchase as well as residual sales on the network that you create should you decide to join the business.

Gary Vincent with network marketing legend
and fellow Agel Team Member Randy Gage

Because there is only a finite amount of money in any given sale, the comp plan is constructed in a way that rewards growth and limits spending excessiveness.

This is most easily understood in a two team structure, or binary model. In a binary, you create two teams: a left and a right, as illustrated in the following diagram:

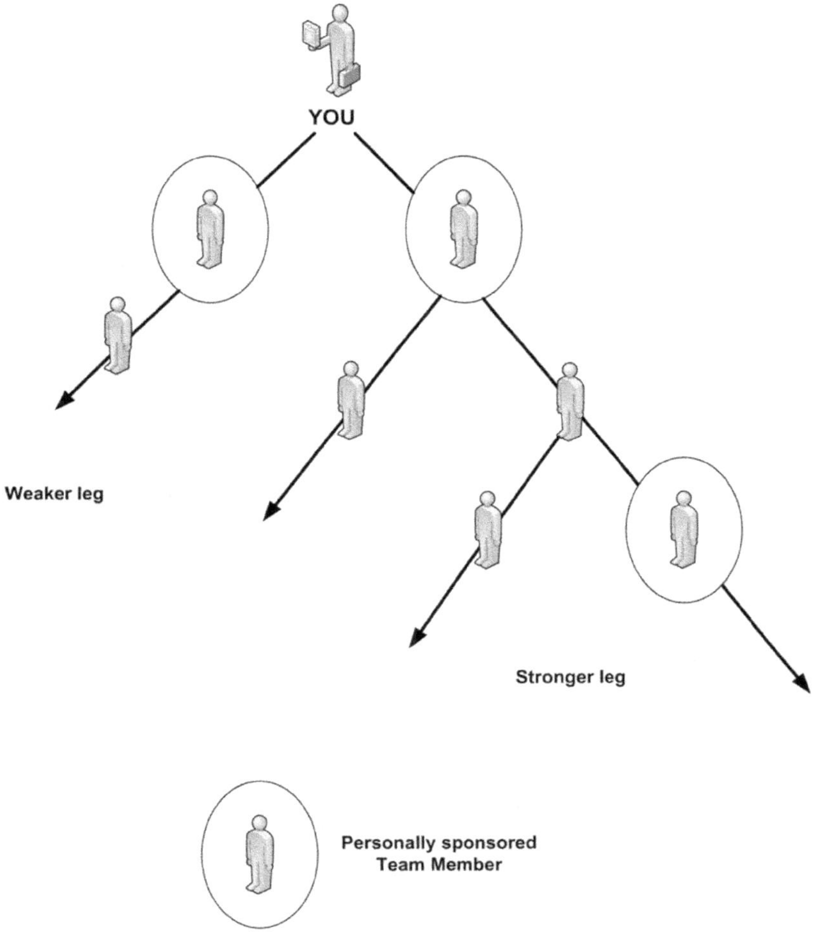

YOU

Weaker leg

Stronger leg

Personally sponsored
Team Member

Typical Binary Genealogy

When you refer someone to the opportunity (or products) and that person joins your team, you become that new person's sponsor. You then place this new customer either in your left team or right team.

Typically, you earn a commission on the new enrollee's initial sale and then an ongoing commission on that person's future business.

Regarding the ongoing commission: in a binary, you are typically paid a percentage of the *entire team's sales* (whether you personally sponsored the members or not). Be aware, however, that you will be paid on the *weaker* team's volume.

This serves two purposes:

1. As a failsafe to guard against overpaying what income is generated.

2. To ensure that the team works as a whole to increase the prosperity of the company.

You may be saying to yourself: wait a second, why am I not paid on the sales of the both teams simultaneously?

The best way to answer this is by example. Suppose you have an item that sells for $10.00 and you earn a team volume commission of 10%. It wouldn't take long before the entire $10.00 is used up and there would not be enough to pay the rest of the individuals or the company.

By paying on the weaker side, this allows a constant strive toward growing the company and keeps commission payouts in check based on the fixed price of the commodity that is being sold.

Most comp plans have other incentives but you get the picture. As new members come in on either side, your entire organization grows.

The beauty of the binary structure is that because there are only two teams, you have an opportunity for 'spill over' members from your upline to be placed into **your** organization.

In other words, your organization can grow by your efforts, your upline's efforts, and your downline's efforts. This is why network marketing is one of the best ways for an average person to become wealthy.

♦♦♦♦

GC: I believe that network marketing is the ideal business model for the small, home-based entrepreneur for a variety of reasons including the following:

1. Low start-up cost.

2. Little or no prior experience is required provided that appropriate training tools are available.

3. Degrees and accreditations are not required.

4. Business hours (and amount) are completely flexible and can accommodate anyone's individual needs.

5. There are literally hundreds of companies using the network marketing business model making it simple for an individual to find a company that shares his/her personal interests.

How to Build Your Network Marketing Business

There are three primary methods for building a home-based network marketing business:

- Traditional home meeting approach
- Candidate prospecting by purchasing leads
- Internet prospecting and promotion

Traditional Home Meeting Approach

The first method of building a network marketing enterprise is the use of personal contacts and home-based meetings in order to provide a business overview and to recruit new partners. The following primary steps need to be taken in order to succeed with this model:

1. Use the product yourself.

This is an essential component for success that is too often overlooked: To properly promote a product or service, you first need to be a consumer of the product. In the industry, this is called "being a product of the product."

By doing so, demonstrates that you have faith in the product, a commitment to its successful growth, and can provide the best testimonial possible: **Your own.**

Personally, I have found it to be much easier to endorse a product when I am also a faithful consumer. This belief (or disbelief if you are not a consumer) in your product can be portrayed through both your verbal and non-verbal communication queues and can often be the difference between a possible sale and a recruitment failure.

2. Treat your endeavor as a business and not as a hobby.

One of the primary reasons for the failure of a home-based business is that people treat their enterprise more like a hobby than a business.

With any worthwhile endeavor, **you must be committed to its success or you will fail.** For most network marketing ventures, I have found that a minimum of 20 hours each week is required in order to both promote the business and maintain proper records. The vast majority of this time (> 80%) needs to be devoted to recruitment.

The best way that I have found to effectively manage this time commitment is to set a weekly schedule that devotes sufficient time to business-related activities.

This is critical, for it has the effect of creating a proper mindset that will directly impact your recruitment performance and has the added benefit of demonstrating your dedication to succeed to prospective clients.

3. Make a list of prospective clients and do not limit your choices.

To give yourself a jump start, begin by making a list of at least 100 persons that you can approach as possible enrollees with your business.

One of the biggest mistakes that I have seen in this area by new recruits in the business is that they limit the number of potential contacts by letting their own preconceptions concerning a person get in the way.

Do not let yourself make this mistake. Do not allow yourself to decide that your business would be right for this person or that another person likely would not be interested. Until you discuss your proposal with a client, you have no idea how the business information will be perceived.

My advice is to let the prospect decide. Also, do not allow yourself to become discouraged if your star prospect – the one that you consider perfect for the opportunity – declines your offer.

I believe that the old saying that there are "more fish in the sea" can be applied in this instance. You can expect more negative than favorable responses for any variety of reasons. DO NOT GET DISCOURAGED. As your skills improve, so will your recruitment ratio.

Lastly, I suggest that you take full advantage of any prepackaged information tools provided by your company. I have found that most successful network marketing companies provide both video and audio tools to be used in the recruitment process.

Do yourself a big favor and allow these tools to do the talking. You should use these audio and video tools extensively because they have been created by marketing experts for the express reason of promoting your business.

4. Conduct business receptions.

After identifying potential prospects from your initial lead list, the final step that you must perform is to conduct a business reception at your home. Inform these candidates that you would like to invite them to an informal reception in which you plan to launch your new enterprise. A strategy that you may wish to consider is the "60 Second Presentation" described later in the book.

Explain that your reception will be an informal gathering in which you plan to show/play materials that will describe your business in detail.

An informal approach is the best to take. By keeping your business meeting informal you will relax both yourself and your prospective clients.

Always point the prospect to the company's marketing materials first. If they still have questions after reviewing them, consider having an up line member available during your home meeting to field their concerns.

A good way to do this is to schedule either a personal appearance or a telephone conference call with the individual that sponsored or introduced the business to you.

This demonstrates that you are operating in a team environment with your sponsor and this technique prevents you from "over selling" the business.

Remember (I mentioned this above, but it bears repeating): you should let the information packages provided by the company do the talking and the majority of the selling.

Candidate Prospecting by Purchasing Leads

The second method of building a successful network marketing business is to purchase screened leads from vendors. Purchasing leads can be of great benefit if you lack a wide range of prospective clients; however there are several aspects that you must consider:

1. How do I purchase leads?

This is perhaps the easiest question to answer. Simply use an Internet search engine and type "network marketing leads" and you will find hundreds of vendor possibilities.

As an additional resource, there are several monthly magazines published regarding new business opportunities that can be an invaluable source of information. This leads us readily to the next question that must be answered:

2. How do I find the best leads?

This is a much tougher question and may require some research on your part to determine the types of leads most valuable to your product and business model.

The leads that you purchase should be chosen carefully. Preferably, your leads should be "real time."

What do I mean by real time?

The leads that you purchase should be as current as possible. There are several internet sources that specialize in real time leads. Simply put, these leads are individuals that have requested information through various media outlets concerning home-based business opportunities. Such sources include blogs, radio ads, recruiting websites, special offers, etc...

Be prepared. Quality leads can be costly and you will find cheap and expensive ones out there. As with most things in life, "you get what you pay for."

By purchasing real time leads, you are more likely to avoid prospects that have been approached numerous times concerning business opportunities. Let's be honest, it is human nature for someone to be less likely to be interested in your business venture if they have been contacted several times recently. You will become just another "seller" that stood in line to pitch your business op.

If you choose to purchase leads that are not real time, be prepared to be disappointed in your results. These are often dated leads and you will invariably waste valuable time contacting individuals that are either no longer interested or have already chosen another business.

3. Now that I have my leads, what do I do with them?

This may sound like a nonsensical question to ask, but would it surprise you to know that most purchased leads are never called.

Why is this?

Leads are purchased for all of the right reasons. You want your business to grow and succeed however, no one likes to fail and this is the precise mentality that causes most leads to sit idle.

If we do not have immediate success when calling leads, we get discouraged and disheartened by our failures.

This ultimately leads to self doubt and ruins our chances to properly promote our business to prospective team members and clients.

What is the answer?

Have a plan of action before you call. By plan of action, I mean a carefully crafted and designed approach that covers everything from your initial introduction and promotion, to your ultimate call backs and close.

I recommend using scripts that cover the most typically encountered questions and situations. RELAX. You do not need to reinvent the wheel. There are several internet vendors that sell a wide variety of scripts that covers this topic. Use any search engine and type "prospecting scripts" and you will find numerous vendors.

Internet Prospecting and Promotion

With the advent of the internet and personal computers, I have often been shocked by the small number of individuals that take full advantage of this tool for marketing home-based businesses. This is probably due to a lack of knowledge and computer savvy.

HomeBizMarketeer

AGELITY INC.

**HomeBizMarketeer.com
to the rescue!**

We designed HomeBizMarketeer.com to solve this dilemma. HomeBizMarketeer.com offers a variety of self study courses and e-books that cover all aspects of internet marketing for home-based entrepreneurs. We discuss a myriad of topics, including:

- How to generate internet traffic to your website.
- Basic website security issues.
- How to get free one way internet links.
- How to get your web-page to the first page during internet searches.
- Using giveaways to create a mailing list.
- Taking advantage of pay for play profits.
- Guides for quickly writing articles.
- How to take advantage of internet marketing.

- Using blogs to generate traffic and promote products.
- Finding and developing profitable niches.
- The basics of email marketing.
- How to attract clients that will continue to use your products and services.
- How to take advantage of private label and master resell rights.
- Writing your own business newsletter.
- Introduction to web page building tools and free internet hosting.
- Taking advantage of joint ventures.
- Plus many, many, more.

So which of the three approaches is the best?

This is up to the individual. If you are most comfortable approaching those within your "inner circle," then the traditional method may be the most suited for your talents.

On the other hand, if you find (as I did) that it is easier to promote a business venture to strangers, then the method of purchasing leads may have merit.

My personal recommendation and preference however, is to use the power of the internet to build my business.

WHY?

If you choose the traditional approach, you always run the substantial risk of losing friends if the business venture fails, or at best, making yourself a social outcast for several years. I have found that the surest way to ruin strong relationships is to bring money into the equation.

I shy away from purchasing leads as well because to a significant degree your success is determined by your ability to conduct direct sales.

There are very few natural born salespersons. Rather, I find that this skill is honed with years of practical experience. Most are naturally skeptical when approached by a stranger and should you choose this business approach, be well prepared to combat this tendency or you will have limited or no success.

My personal choice is to use the internet tools described in this chapter in order to build my business. With the internet, you can literally present your product to millions of potential clients quickly and efficiently utilizing creative marketing and distribution techniques. I highly recommend that anyone considering starting network marketing businesses consider the internet as their primary choice because, simply put, it is the way of the future.

VII. Network Marketing: Techniques For Success

GV: As with any business but particularly with network marketing, the key to your success is prospecting, following up, and enrolling. If you have ever been involved with a network marketing company and did not experience the results you had hoped for, it was probably a weakness in one or more of these critical areas.

However, true success doesn't stop there. You have to be able to lead in a manner that creates duplication in your downline. This is the step most people miss. You may have a terrific skill in getting people sponsored into the business, but if you cannot achieve duplication, you will eventually burn out.

I remember my school days sitting in a class room and mentally wishing that the teacher would hurry up and get to the point. "Just give me the answer and I'll be on my way," I'd think to myself. I have come to realize, however, that sometimes you have to go through the *theory* in order to truly get the point; else you may not be prepared to handle the circumstances you are faced with that foster success.

This chapter is one of those theory chapters that you can't afford to skip if you really want to grasp the nuts and bolts of thinking like a winner. Yes, we will describe some advanced strategies in future chapters to help you accelerate your wealth much faster than normal, but you need to get the foundation laid first. Believe me: you don't want to try to fly the jet without first building the runway!

Creating Your Game Plan

Just as in life, success in network marketing greatly depends on defining your purpose and seizing every moment of opportunity that you have. Now that you know what network marketing is, we would like to share with you some proven techniques that will help improve your own chances for success.

Our goal here is to help you establish a clear direction and purpose for your business, a blueprint if you will, that will help you build that successful dynasty in network marketing.

Define your "Why"

This might sound simple, but it is so very important. The greater the *why*, the stronger the *how.* If your why is, "I want to be successful in network marketing so that I can quit my job," that is too vague. You need to be specific with you goals.

You also shouldn't be too hard on yourself either; success does take time. For example, let's say you are currently earning $48,000 per year in your job. If you are wanting to transition from this job to your network marketing 'job', then you have to first identify that you need to have the skill to make at least $4000 per month (the equivalent of one month's income at $48K annually.)

Go a step further and take it to the week. Ask yourself, "What would making an extra $1000 per week allow me to do?" Take out a sheet of paper and answer this. The more reasons why, the more likely you are to accomplish this small task. Be clear about your why. Clarity equals results.

Next ask yourself, "How many people do I personally need to sponsor into my business to make $1000.00?"

Think about this: what you focus on, you create. That which you focus on expands and you gain power over it.

Commit to the smallest goal, work on it, make mistakes, be open to try new things, and keep working until you achieve it. Repeat this process and most importantly, don't ever give up when things are not going your way; try something different, but do not outright quit. Quitting is the only sure way to fail.

Remember Your Priorities. When defining your why, remember your priorities. This subtle step may help you avoid frustration in the long run. Is the reason for starting a home-based business to spend more time with your family?

If so, be sure to include them at the beginning and keep them in the picture! It will serve you no good if you trade one 'job' for another and leave out what is important to you.

One can easily become absorbed in the business and be too busy for the people and life fulfilling things that matter most. Don't let this happen to you. If you set concrete guidelines that **are in line with your priorities** you are less likely to circumvent them when 'the business calls.'

Let me give you an example of priorities in practice. Say you want to spend more time with family. Be sure that you and your spouse define when you are going to work on the business and when you are not.

If Fridays are your date night, be unwavering not to do business on Fridays. Don't take calls, don't schedule business briefings, don't stay in front of the computer –

go out with your spouse and be there for that person.

Similarly, set specific times for your business and be congruent here as well. If you commit 2 hours each day to the business, set aside a specific time and **work your business during that time**. Keep distractions away from work. If your network marketing time is from 6PM – 8PM, don't watch TV or zone out during this time, work the business.

If you are holding a home meeting, be sure there is a babysitter for the kids. Keep the pets out of your living room and do not take personal calls during your meetings. Be 100% present in what you do.

You will know you are successful if your business is in line with your priorities. Knowing this upfront will help keep your business on track and create a better sense of harmony in what you are trying to accomplish in life. If there is a lack of harmony or a conflict between your priorities and your business, one or both will suffer. If this happens, you risk losing your business or worse, what matters most to you.

Create a Mission Statement

Businesses big and small have mission statements to give them a sense of direction and purpose. Do you? Now that you have a why, consider writing a one or two sentence mission statement that describes your purpose.

Here is an example:

> "It is my mission to improve the health and well being of others through my opportunity. By doing so I will increase my wealth by $4000.00 per month until I have doubled my income, and will spend more time with family, helping them to succeed as well."

Your mission statement can change from time to time as goals are accomplished and priorities change, but keeping them defined will have you on your way to achieving your goals.

Attitude is Everything

Struggle is part of success. You cannot hope for life to be easy and most real endeavors, most real accomplishments, are the result of multiple failures, challenges, and hardships that were overcome. Volumes can be written about the power of positive thinking. Having your "why" is one thing, but being positive through the good times and bad is what will keep you going. Plus, the degree of success you *enjoy* in this business and in life will be in direct proportion to your attitude.

Henry Ford was one of the world's best known entrepreneurs. He is famous for the Model-T and for saying, "If you think you can do a thing or think you can't do a thing, you're right." In other words, what you say to yourself – your attitude – will ultimately determine your outcome.

Here are some keys to keeping a positive attitude:

Limit Complaining. This reminds me of Proverbs 21:9:

> "Better to live alone in a tumbledown shack than share a mansion with a nagging spouse." -- *from "The Message"*

A lot can be taken from this. You won't want to do it if you're complaining about it (or your family is complaining about it.) Love what you do and learn from your mistakes.

Be Thankful. Be genuinely grateful for what you have and more will be given to you. The universe just works this way. Also, be thankful to others and what they bring to your life. Think about your family, friends, and co-workers and remember to thank them for the little things they do. Be present and aware, even in the littlest of moments; be genuine. The sheer fact that you are alive is cause for thankfulness.

The fact that you have the opportunity to read this now and experience a richer, more fulfilling life is cause for thankfulness. Have you told your spouse or your child how much you love them or how much they mean to you today?

Be Contagious. I'm not talking about spreading a cold. I'm saying that a good attitude is contagious. Make a conscious effort to be happy and to reflect that happiness to those around you.

This sometimes takes work and I acknowledge that we cannot always be happy all of the time. We can however live in a state of awareness and be happy most of the time. As network marketing revolves around duplication, your happy attitude is needed for your downline. Just as negativity and doubt can duplicate, so can happiness and an optimistic outlook on life.

Practice Generosity. Are you a cheerful giver? Random acts of kindness are in short supply these days and YOU have the opportunity to show the world that you care.

Whether it be your time or money, donate something of yourself to help others. You will be amazed at how good you feel and the blessings you personally will experience.

Take a Skills Inventory

Take out a sheet of paper and draw a vertical line down the center. Next, ask yourself: "What are my strengths and what are my weaknesses?" Write down your strengths on the left of the page and your weaknesses on the right.

Too often, we focus on our strengths. However, it is our weaknesses that will ultimately determine whether or not our business will work. It is here that we need to improve and here where we need to focus. Again, be as clear as possible and make yourself *aware* of these. Look for ways to improve in these areas and do not ignore them.

Now take a look at your strengths. Are you a 'people person' or an introvert? Understanding this upfront will help you decide which model will work for you. For example, if you don't like talking to people, then purchasing leads and cold calling them on the phone will probably not work *for you*. You will find a dozen and one excuses not to pick up the phone or at least procrastinate until the lead goes from cold to 'not a snowball's chance in hell.'

Conversely, perhaps you are a computer person. You like technology and would like to start your business online. Knowing this will help you identify an automated systems approach to get you best married up with your strengths.

It's Not About The Money

Business philosopher Jim Rohn once said, "We generally change ourselves for one of two reasons: inspiration or desperation." Superficially, we may fool ourselves into thinking that, "If I just had more money, everything will be fine."

However, the sooner you realize that it's not about the money, the sooner you'll be able to make lots of it. Network marketing is about skills and leverage; money is a byproduct. Improve your skills and the money will follow.

Ambition and the willingness to learn are far more valuable than having the funds to get started. In fact, you are far more likely to lose big if you go into an endeavor with plenty of capital and no skill. In network marketing, more so than other business models (like real estate, securities investing, etc.), this is especially true.

So, setting money aside, what else do you need? You must have enthusiasm, faith, and determination.

Your contagious attitude (enthusiasm), belief in your opportunity (faith), and resiliency to stay with the program until you achieve results (determination) are keys to your success.

Time is also important. You must be willing to set aside time each week for the business and for self development. No matter what you do, these two things cannot be ignored.

Many people get lured into network marketing with the belief that they can work part time and earn a full time income. While this is true *later in the game* you have to give the business the time necessary to build it.

Go back to your why; remember in the example of a person working 40 hours a week to earn $48K per year? If a person is working a FULL TIME job to earn this living, some time is necessary to match this with network marketing. Think about it and you'll see it just makes common sense.

You also need to devote time to the discipline of self development. One book, CD, seminar, etc. is not enough. This is a lifelong process. Never stop learning.

It is ultimately skill that will allow you to build wealth and keep it, far more than money in this business.

Be the Right Person

Personality is so very important in network marketing. Think about it: do you want to do business with a sour puss? Even if your business is solely on the Internet, your personality bleeds through.

Whether you are a pleasant person by nature or not, you must become one; you must become the type of person that you would like to do business with.

You must be approachable. Can others come to you with questions and concerns? Can they look to you for advice? Does your leadership inspire others to become like you? You are the example that others will follow.

Run Your Business, Don't Let Your Business Run You!

A successful leader knows how to manage time. We all have only 24 hours in a day. If you don't run your business, it will take control of your life. Below are some tips on helping you in this:

Keep your phone calls short and to the point. Network marketers are notorious for long-winded phone calls. However, what most people don't get is: it is not the quantity of the speech, but the quality. Don't rattle on and on.

Don't always answer the phone. This might sound counterproductive to operating a successful business, but hear me out. So many people are so tied to their cell phones that they don't know how *not to answer them!*

I was in the grocery store the other day and this woman had her hands full of stuff at the checkout line. In the middle of the purchase, she took a call right when she was paying and interacting with the clerk.

The clerk (and the rest of us in line) had to stand by and wait as she carried on this phone conversation. How much more courteous it would have been had she just waited another 60 seconds until her purchase was complete to answer the call.

Expanding on this: if you let a phone call interrupt your dinner, your business is running you, not the other way around. If you let a phone call interrupt love making with your spouse, then the business is running you.

Phone call management should be a priority. Think about it this way, do phone calls ever come when it is convenient? No! They always come when you mind is on something else. You could be driving, eating, in the middle of a speech, but rarely do they come when you are at your desk, in your zone, and ready to tackle the subject at hand.

My advice: let the call go to voice mail and call everybody back who left messages at the same time every day *when you are mentally prepared to talk on the phone.*

Establish set times and do your best not to deviate. This is especially true with your meetings. If the start time is 7PM, start at 7PM. It is rude for the people who are at your meeting to have to wait on those who are late or may not show up at all. Equally important, don't let your meetings go over. Many of the people have set times, babysitters, etc. Be respectful of their schedules.

Carry a Day Planner. The best way to know what's going on is to use a day planner. Be organized and know what you are going to do each day. Do your best to allocate set times for the tasks and work within those times.

Though this is not always possible, it will help

you better control the situations that you face.

Follow A System

Although I am all for trial and error,

especially when you're just getting started,

there is really no need to reinvent the wheel.

Network marketing has been around over half a

century and there are solid, proven systems in

place.

Remember that you are trying to build a

network, or a team. Thus you need to look at

what system will allow your team to thrive.

Keep in mind that duplication may be a factor

in this. Does your system allow many people to

do a few simple things, or is your approach renegade and hard to duplicate?

One of the unique differences of network marketing over traditional sales is that the customers are the members of the network. Thus, you need to be able to illustrate to your team a way for them to succeed. You need to be a leader and they, in turn, need to be leaders of their teams.

Systemization is a way to achieve duplication. It is one thing to enroll a new team member into the business. It is another to keep him or her there and turn that person into a leader. Ideally, you should align yourself with a business that already has a proven system in place that you can share with your team. If you do not, then you will need to create one.

The purpose of systemization is to take the focus off you and put it on the system. Remember, alone you can only achieve so much, with others you can achieve so much more. Getting everybody to do some repeatable small things can take you much further then you being the star of the show.

A chief reason for failure in network marketing is often the lack of a system. Because it is relatively cheap to get into a home-based business, many people are attracted to the industry.

However, many people don't know how to succeed and are quickly discouraged. You do not want to have high attrition (drop outs) in your team. If everybody has a system to follow, their chances of success are far more likely. And, of course, the more successful teammates you have, the more successful you will become!

Get To Manager

Every major network marketing opportunity has names for their different ranks. For our purposes, I will use the term "Manager."

When I bring someone into the business, my goal is to get them to Manager within the first month. It is statistically proven that one must achieve success early or that person will become disappointed and eventually drop out.

With a new recruit, your window is no more than three months, but if you can get them to manager within the first month, they are excited and will want to continue. You can measure the effectiveness and replicability of your system based on the number of people who can get to their first rank advancement.

K.I.S.S.

Keep it simple, stupid! Your system should be very easy to follow. Don't expect your team to follow something that takes a rocket scientist to figure out. Appeal to the masses. Ask yourself, "Can success be achieved in a predictable manner if the person sticks with the program?"

Introduce, follow-up, recruit. Does your system do these things?

FORM Your Prospects

This might sound arrogant, but people only care about themselves. The sooner you realize this, the more likely you will be able to experience positive results.

When you are recruiting a new prospect, do not talk about yourself or the company at first. FORM your prospect first. FORM is an acronym for Family, Occupation, Recreation, and Money. The more people talk about themselves, the more they will *sell themselves* on your opportunity!

In the FORM model, you transverse topics

by letting the prospect do the talking. Be careful not to interrupt the prospect, definitely be mindful enough not to start spilling the beans about yourself and your company!

As the prospect begins to talk about his or her family, occupation, things they like to do for fun, and his or her monetary situation, *listen.* The prospect will reveal a lot about his/herself as you begin to FORM the conversation.

You will learn that person's interests, needs, and financial status. You will learn what motivates that person and what things would make him or her happy.

◆◆◆◆

The 60 Second Presentation

GC: One last technique that I would like to discuss regarding network marketing is the use of a 60 second presentation to quickly and concisely present your business opportunity.

Why is this so important?

How often do you feel that there are simply not enough hours in a given day to get all of your daily duties completed? If your answer is: Almost daily. Then you can readily see the importance of this topic.

Most individuals that are new to the network marketing business make the classic mistake of doing a 'data dump' on the prospect. They throw all of the facts related to their company's history, product line, and opportunity at new prospects in such a way that the prospect is overwhelmed by the information and immediately chooses to avoid the opportunity.

To put it another way, most of us (myself included) do not like to be sold anything. When is the last time that you responded positively to a telephone call from a telemarketer or relished the thought of visiting a car lot and talking with the salesman?

So what do we do to avoid the possibility of alienating new prospective clients? There is a simple solution. You say the following:

"I can give you a complete presentation, but it would take a full sixty seconds.

When could you set aside sixty seconds?"

Are you surprised? Don't be.

When you are talking to a new prospect for your business, say the following: "I have a great new opportunity for you". If you note their facial expression, you will immediately see negative nonverbal signs.

Why? Your prospect is now expecting a sales pitch. To avoid this negative response, simply say "*I can give you a complete presentation, but it would take a full sixty seconds. When could you set aside sixty seconds?*"

You may be surprised that nearly 100% of the time you get a positive response similar too "How about now!" If you find this hard to believe, try this technique as an experiment and determine your results.

But you might ask "What can I possibly say in one minute?" A lot. One minute is enough time to state a few essential facts regarding your business, allows your prospect to answer yes or no, allows for one or two questions to be asked, and most importantly, will be over quickly.

The key to this technique is to say the right things that allows someone to make a decision. In my experience, there are 3 major factors that most people need or want to know:

1. What kind of business is this?
2. How much can I expect to make if I get involved?
3. What do I have to do to generate a paycheck?

These are the root topics that need to be addressed. If you are taking longer, this is a sign that you are providing more information than is needed at the initial introductory stage.

Let's face it: all you really need to determine initially is if someone would actually be interested in the opportunity. Most of the other related facts can be discussed during training sessions.

Having said this, what do we discuss during our 60 seconds?

Here is a real world example that I have seen used and that has proven to be successful regarding a company involved in the nutritional supplement business:

"If you would like to earn an extra $5,000 per month, you need to be able to do these four things:

"Number One, don't change. Continue recommending or promoting things like you always have, like a baby sitter, or movie, or favorite TV show. Continue recommending things you like.

"Number Two, we're in the nutrition business. We have this wonderful supplement that you rip and sip and a natural skin care line. Using these products can help you look and feel younger, and the best part, they cost less than $3 per day to use.

"Number Three, sometime in your lifetime, you have to find four people who feel the same way about this business that you do. They want to earn a full time income or really good part time income.

Now, you don't have to find all four right away. It can be one a week, one a month, one a decade. But sometime in your **lifetime**, find four people who feel like you do.

"And, Number Four. Between you, and everybody you talk to, and everybody that they talk to, and everybody that they talk to, forever and ever and ever, you eventually accumulate about 300 people that use the supplements regularly. And then you'd earn an extra $5,000 per month.

That's all there is! What do you think?

See how easy that was? All you have to do at this point is listen for one of the three responses that you will most likely receive:

1. "That sounds ok, how do I get started?"

Answer: Say something similar to the following:

"Every Thursday evening we have a little meeting at my house. You can come over and pick up your kit, meet some other members, see how they are doing, and see how far ahead you're going to get.

"Or if you're in a hurry, we can go online to my website and fill in your application."

If you are new and not sure, you can say: "I'm really not sure, let me call up my sponsor and he can walk us through it so you can get started right away..." You get the picture.

2. "I'm not interested."

Answer: "That's okay."

You have your answer, so move on to another topic.

3. "That doesn't sound too bad, but I need to know more."

Answer: Provide a response to their question in about 30 seconds or less. End the conversation with "What do you think?"

**This is simple and straight to the point. Try it.
You will be amazed by your success.**

VIII. Network Marketing: Tying It All Together

GC: In the preceding chapters, we have discussed the primary ways of building a network marketing business. But there remains one very important topic that has not been discussed.

There are hundreds of network marketing 'opportunities' in the world today. With such a large number of biz ops to pick from, you might be asking yourself:

How do I chose the right one and make it work for me? We will now answer this question.

Choosing the Right Company.

I am a firm believer that you learn as much, or more, from a failure than a success. With this in mind, I will now relate the criteria that I use to evaluate a network marketing opportunity based primarily on lessons learned from past experience. I will show you how to be a critical judge of facts and I will show you the ways to spot the scams that pervade the marketplace today.

No matter what your reasons may be for getting involved in network marketing, the two largest factors for most are time freedom and tax advantages. With these two goals in mind, it is imperative that the company with which you chose to align yourself with supports these factors.

How many people do you know trade their standard 9-to-5 job for the chance to start their own business, only to find that their own business takes even more of their time? If this is the case, then you need to find another vocation.

Most small businesses fail within their first year for a wide variety of reasons and network marketing is no exception. Many people become involved in network marketing because of the low start-up cost and the little or no experience that is required.

How many people do you know that have become involved in network marketing, failed, and now foster negativity toward the business model? They believe it to be some type of scam when in fact it is completely legitimate and viable.

The primary source of failure is that **they** failed to choose the correct opportunity to meet their expected goals (or maybe they failed to follow the prescribed steps needed to be successful).

Five Types of Biz Ops

There are 5 basic types of opportunities that you will encounter:

The Gangbuster

The first type is the gangbuster (or Ponzi). These are the true scams. In this scenario, the opportunity appears to be viable and sound – in fact, too good to be true. Funds pour in at an outstanding rate.

However, this is but an illusion. These types of operations are invariably stopped by law enforcement agencies and are more commonly known as pyramid schemes.

Examples of these include certain investment clubs, chain letters, recipe clubs, gas pills, airplane games, and many others. Recognize them to be plots for the people that created them to move money to the top of the structure.

Let's be very clear here: The gangbuster is an illegal scam and is not a legitimate network marketing company. They defraud and hurt individuals and are to be avoided.

The Established Giant

The second type is the established mature company. These are legitimate companies that have had tremendous past success over many years. They have become industry giants and generate billions in sales annually.

Unfortunately, their success is also their undoing. They have become so large that the opportunities for new distributors to develop legacy income producing streams is limited or non-existent.

The chance of "cashing-in" on the company's exponential growth is in the past.

The Drifter

The third type is the drifter. A drifter company has often been in existence for many years, but has failed to experience true exponential growth. The only true growth that these companies experience is when they open a new market or introduce a new product.

Drifters use their track record of longevity as a recruitment tool and constantly proclaim that their growth spurt is right around the corner. Don't be fooled. The growth spurt will never happen. If the company were truly on the fast track, they would have already reached the mature company stage.

In this type of opportunity, it is impossible to generate legacy income positions unless you are willing to stick-it-out for decades.

The Seller

The fourth is the true "seller" model. In this type of company, you must continually sell, sell, sell in order to make any income. By their nature, they are designed to be small business models and do not afford the opportunity to develop large teams that produce legacy income positions.

Would it surprise you to know that about 90 percent of the total population are considered to be non-sales types? Based on this statistic, it is easy to see that 90 percent of the people that adopt this approach will fail.

People in this broad category, including myself, do not relish the idea of peddling products to someone. I also don't enjoy the astronomically high rejection rate that comes with this job.

Most persons in this scenario will use the product themselves, show it to their inner circle of family and friends, but will never be comfortable in marketing their product to strangers. This type of company is primarily for the true salesperson; that smaller, 10 percent of the population.

The Up and Coming Giant

The final type of company that I will discuss are those that are truly destined for future greatness: The Up and Coming Giant. These are the companies that have the greatest chance to become the next billion dollar mega success and have the best chance for the development of legacy income positions.

Locating an Up and Coming Giant

Gary and I have studied companies that fall into this category and they have several things in common:

1. A Flashy and Consumable Product Line

The best types of products for long term financial success in network marketing are consumables. Your business will continue within the network because the product is being used (consumed) then needs reordered. Makeup and nutritional supplements tend to fit the bill pretty well in the consumables line.

Additionally, the product needs to be easy to understand. If you need a doctoral degree in physics to understand the concept, it will never work. You must be able to explain your product and its benefits in under a minute or it will seem to be too complicated.

As I mentioned in the title to this section, you need to have a flashy and consumable product **line**. One of the other shocking truths is that one-product companies don't hold their own over the long term.

Like the non-consumables, they can create some initial excitement. But there simply is not enough volume produced to sustain the compensation plan and reward top leaders. At some point they recognize that distributors in other companies with the same size organization make substantially more money than they do. So even if they love their product and their company, they ultimately make a business decision and choose to build a business elsewhere. This has been demonstrated countless times in the last decade with the dozens of magic fruit juice companies.

2. Proper Capitalization

This one is pretty simple: does the company have enough money to compete globally and handle the growth that comes from bringing on new markets?

Look for a company with a management that has a global vision. A company literally needs millions in today's world as factories, research and development, and distribution channels are brought online.

Ensure that the company's executive management team is able to raise the capital they need, either through private banking or by partnering with venture capitalists.

3. Management Depth

The Management of a given network marketing company must also have experience. Look at what these individuals have accomplished in the past as an indicator of their ability to perform positively in the future.

Can the leadership build the foundation of company support that offers you the best chance to reach your goals? Do they have an all-star team of professionals to take the company to the top echelon of the industry?

4. A Compensation Plan that Provokes the Correct Behavior.

Since the Network Marketing industry began in the late 1950s, compensation plans have evolved to keep pace with the changing market conditions. Plans that worked great in the 1970s didn't necessarily perform well in the 1980s. And plans that served well in the 1990s often don't pass the market demands of today.

A good compensation plan will incorporate the very best elements of the older plans of legitimate businesses, but leave out the limiting characteristics of each.

Specifically what to watch for:

- People never break away from you,
- Your volume is not "washed" weekly, and
- It keeps a larger portion of your group within your pay range.

Your compensation plan should include fast start money when you begin, transitional income as you grow the network, and residual security once your group is built.

5) Field Leadership

No company can put itself into momentum. This has to be created by the field leadership – the people who are actually in the trenches, recruiting, training, and supporting the team. As you look for a network marketing opportunity, consider this element to be YOU.

Once you have determined that you have found an up and coming giant, you will still need the following in order to succeed:

A System

Is there a step-by-step system for you to follow? No matter what your education level, experience, or age, is there something for you to follow?

A good leader will know the best ways to build a network and will create a system utilizing this, so everyone has the same opportunity for success.

An Infrastructure For The System

An important element of a system is having the proper infrastructure in place. Type 5 companies with strong leadership will have powerful recruiting materials such as magazines, DVDs, audios, websites and many other marketing materials in place. These resources allow you to get started fast, even if you have never been in the business before.

Training

A final and often overlooked aspect of success is training. How do you use the systems in place? Are there weekly Leadership Training Calls, webcasts, local, regional, and international training events? Are there annual events to offer you high-level training on how to build your team and create a true residual income and lasting wealth?

If you have answered yes to the above, then it looks like you are ready to get started. If you haven't yet found your Type 5 opportunity, then I would strongly encourage you to wait until such an opportunity arises.

I waited, did my due diligence, and when the right company came that included all of the above success tracks previously mentioned, joined. Now, I couldn't be happier.

Based on my criteria, what company did I choose?

AGEL ENTERPRISES

Agel receives a Grade "A" in all areas that we used to evaluate a network marketing opportunity. For your benefit, we have included a case study on this company below. In full disclosure, Gary and I are both team members in Agel.

AGEL CASE STUDY[1]

Agel was evaluated under the following criteria:

- Low cost of entry
- Low on-going costs
- Low risk of failure
- High residual income potential and
- Ideal timing both in the marketplace and in the company's growth.

In this study, you will learn why:

- Agel takes advantage of the convergence of three mega-trends in the world.
- Agel introduces a revolutionary new delivery mechanism for tried and true, universally appealing products.
- Agel assembled a "Dream Team" of experienced executives and leaders.
- Agel provides this opportunity to you at the most ideal time.
- Agel developed a compensation plan and business model designed to reward you with a stable residual income.
- Agel shows you the way to succeed with advanced tools, marketing methods, personal support and in-depth training.

---

[1] Some portions came courtesy of WhyAgel.com. To visit our team-specific page on WhyAgel, visit **www.AgelDreamTeam.US**.

Agel is at the focal point of three mega-growth trends: Health & Wellness, Home-based businesses, and Network Marketing.

The **Health & Wellness** industry is predicted to grow to over $1 TRILLION dollars by 2010.

Home-based businesses give people the opportunity for financial independence and personal freedom. More and more are being started each day.

The **Network Marketing** advertising and distribution model saves companies millions of dollars each year and many new (and old) companies are turning to this model.

The Health & Wellness Industry will grow by $750 BILLION over the next 5 years.

Positioning yourself in the path of a major growth industry is key to a highly successful business.

Right now, the health and wellness industry is a **$250 Billion Industry** and analysts predict it will grow to over **$1 Trillion** dollars annually by the year 2010. This will generate over $1.9 million dollars every 60 seconds. Whether you are involved or not, this is going to happen.

Agel operates within the **direct distribution component** (products delivered directly to consumers) of this industry which is estimated to grow from its current level of **$75 Billion** to around **$300 Billion** by 2010. Within this sector an **increase of $225 Billion** will be generated between now and 2010. If Agel were to capture only one half of one percent of this growth **Agel will be a $1 Billion company.**

Revolutionary new products allow Agel to take advantage of its ideal market positioning and timing.

The world is facing a serious **health challenge** right now. People aren't getting the nutrition their bodies need through their diet. The **empty calories** we eat provide fat, but not much nutrition. Our bodies are crying out for **true nourishment.**

Agel's research into **nutrient delivery** led to the **breakthrough** of suspension gel technology. It's not about another "super pill" or "magic juice"; it's a change in the **delivery mechanism.**

Agel's products are changing the way people take nutritionals and **maintain and improve** their health. It's about tried and true nutritional supplements in a **more potent and convenient form**.

The world is facing a nutrition-based health crisis. Poor nutrition costs billions of dollars and is killing us one bite at a time!

Pills, powders and juices are not the answer.

Study after study has shown that many vitamin and mineral supplements simply **pass through** your body - providing you with limited or even no nutrients.

*The Problem: your body simply can't **assimilate** the nutrition it needs from some pills, capsules and tablets.*

Also, many children and elderly people have extreme **difficulty swallowing** pills. Others choose not to because of the **inconvenience**, and bad smell. Others complain of upset stomachs, the dreadful taste and "vitamin burps." And for people on the go, needing to take water with the pills is a **hassle**.

Powders fare no better. Ever try to mix up a diet or nutritional shake while sitting down at a restaurant - you feel **stupid** and it's **messy**. Or how about while driving your car. That could end your health problems **real quick**!

Or what about those "magic potions," the juices from every unknown bean and berry on the planet. Sure many of them have wonderful benefits, but did you ever try **lugging** a wine bottle with you all day long. They just don't fit in to our **lifestyle**.

But probably the biggest challenge for most people is **not knowing** what supplements they should take - and which ones to choose from the 1000s of brands on display in the store, pharmacy or supermarket.

People are confused and don't know who to **trust**. Store clerks are rarely any help, having no idea themselves. **But a recent technological breakthrough is changing all that.**

Agel's research into nutrient delivery led to the breakthrough of suspension gel technology.

Recently, the scientists at Agel Enterprises reached a technological breakthrough in nutrition, with the introduction of their suspension gel technology.

Elite tri-athletes and marathon runners have been experimenting for several **years** with small packets of gel, looking for a timely blast of energy. Agel researches wondered if this same concept would work for daily consumption of **critical components** like antioxidants, vitamins and minerals.

This led the Agel researchers and scientists to develop Agel's **proprietary suspension gel technology**. By suspending the nutrients in a gel and packaging it in convenient individual servings, Agel's innovative new gel packs let consumers get their **nutrition** on the run.

This new scientific breakthrough in nutrient delivery and assimilation is **revolutionizing the wellness industry.**

There are four critical factors that influence the efficiency of any nutritional supplements you take:
- **Properly timed** ingestion
- **Correct quantities** of nutritional components
- **High bioavailability** of the nutrients
- And the most critical factor: YOU'VE GOT TO ACTUALLY **TAKE** THEM!

Agel Products - A Better Way

The Agel product line truly represents **a better way** to take nutritional supplements, but what does this mean for **you**?

As you evaluate the Agel business opportunity, there is another **very important** factor to consider: Agel's suspension gel technology creates an entirely **new product category**. And history has shown that the **market leaders** who create such categories enjoy a **major share** of that market. And that offers a very lucrative **financial opportunity** for those involved!

Wellness is the **hottest trend** out there today, and now you've got **wellness in a gel pack**! An Agel Team Member has the chance to build a thriving business in this hot new product category.

There are six product factors that are required for a **truly lucrative business opportunity**:

- A **high quality product** that produces measurable results. - No "magic beans" or "blind faith," just time tested, scientifically proven results.
- A **"sizzle" product** that creates buzz. - A product that people will talk about.
- People **"get" the product** concept easily. - It has to be something we can all quickly understand and relate to.
- There is a **real need**, and the product meets the need. - The bigger the need the more potential. Agel = Huge Potential

- A **universal need** for the product. - Not a product for men or women only, or just people in the US, but all ages, all races, all nationalities worldwide.
- **Unique, exclusive** products with proprietary formulas and processes. - Agel's revolutionary idea and pending patents secure the market opportunity.

Agel, as a company, has the ability and talent to capitalize on both the ideal market opportunity and these revolutionary new products.

Every start-up needs to be **properly capitalized**, but few really are. In fact, undercapitalization is the leading cause of failure for new businesses. The Agel founders knew that it would be critical for Agel to have **financial backing** to overcome any unexpected market challenges and persevere. And their vision of such broad-based **international expansion** would take an extraordinary amount of capital. But they were committed to offering the Agel vision **worldwide**.

So they sought the partnership of a **strong and secure funding source.** That was achieved and Agel entered the market with the financial clout to **dominate markets**, expand aggressively and provide the **support team** you need for success.

For more on this Agel case study, the business opportunity, or to join our Dream Team, visit **www.AgelDreamTeam.US**.

IX.   Agile Accelerators

In this chapter we will describe advanced strategies to accelerate your network marketing business. Whether you choose to *join our Agel Dream Team* or set out with your own company, these strategies when used correctly will produce results much faster than any single isolated technique that is traditionally taught.

These strategies are not for the average network marketer, but considering that you are reading this book, you obviously are looking for something more. Thus these are for you.

The Impending Large Event

GC: The impending large event is a coordinated effort to ally yourself with fellow team members to perform mass recruiting drives.

In its most basic form, each current team member agrees to approach as many new potential prospects as possible in an effort to persuade those interested to attend a gathering at a local venue of likeminded individuals.

GV: The Impending Large Event is foreshadowed by a series of smaller events that lead up to it. The first is known as a **Private Business Reception**, or PBR for short.

The PBRs are typically small, in-house meetings done throughout your organization by the individual team members. These usually occur on a weekly basis.

During a PBR, new prospects are given the chance to preview the business opportunity. The preview can be either a DVD, live speech by the host, or a call in from the upline/sponsor. I would recommend not to make the presentation yourself, especially if your company has a DVD or other automated format that you can use.

The PBR should be considered a friendly and informal way for your prospect to learn about the business.

The PBRs will lead into a larger meeting known as a **Business Briefing**, or BB for short.

During a BB, higher-ups from the organization meet with team members and prospects that have been assembled from the PBRs.

Usually those attending the BBs have already expressed an interest in the company and are attending to learn more. In the BB, there may be teleconferences or live presentations from the company or the team's upline leadership.

The BB provides a lead in for a **Super Saturday**, or a major event held usually on a weekend.

During a Super Saturday, multiple teams converge and usually a company representative will be there to conduct training.

As with each progressively larger meeting, there is a recruiting drive to get more and more people to the next larger event.

The result: the entire team is focused on a short-term goal of the next meeting and each member can stay the term and re-energize when they make it to their next bigger event.

If the company is growing and strong, the Super Saturday leads into even larger quarterly events held regionally around the world. At these conferences, thousands are in attendance and the energy is through the roof.

Most who attend become leaders in the organization, as they gain the skills needed to equip them in the next phase of growing their business.

◆◆◆◆

The use of the Impending Large Event (such as the Quarterly Conferences) allows the team to conduct a centralized mass group presentation that leverages the talents of all current team members in the campaign.

It is also often the case that if a large volume of potential prospects can be attracted to a given event, the sponsor of the event, you, can contact company representatives to attend the promotional campaign to promote your business. This has been proven to be very successful in the past in larger urban areas.

Power Leg

GV: The Power Leg is a acceleration technique employed in Binary network marketing models.

In a Power Leg, members are placed in the lowest left or lowest right side of the structure by the sponsor and the sponsor's upline.

The new team member is then required to put forth his/her own efforts to create growth in the weaker side.   To better understand this concept, let me give you an example:

Let's say that I enroll George into my network marketing business. I tell George that I will place him in my lower left side. As I only have a left and a right side, everybody that I place in the Power Leg Left Side will automatically fall under Geroge, thus growing his team while simultaneously growing mine.

In this way we can both help each other. This is how we set up our Agel Dream Team:

When a person enrolls as a new team member at **www.AgelDreamTeam.US**, I become their sponsor and they are automatically enrolled in George's downline.

Similarly, when George enrolls somebody, that person is placed in his power leg: bottom left or bottom right. In my illustration, whenever George places a person in his left power leg, me, everybody that I placed on my left team (George included), and everybody that enrolled via the website benefits!

While I am building this left power leg, my right is being automatically built by my upline (which originated in California and now spans throughout the world.) As these teams develop, I can focus on my left side growing the power leg indefinitely deep.

Should the left surpass the right, I can switch and begin growing the right power leg. The process cycles back and forth.

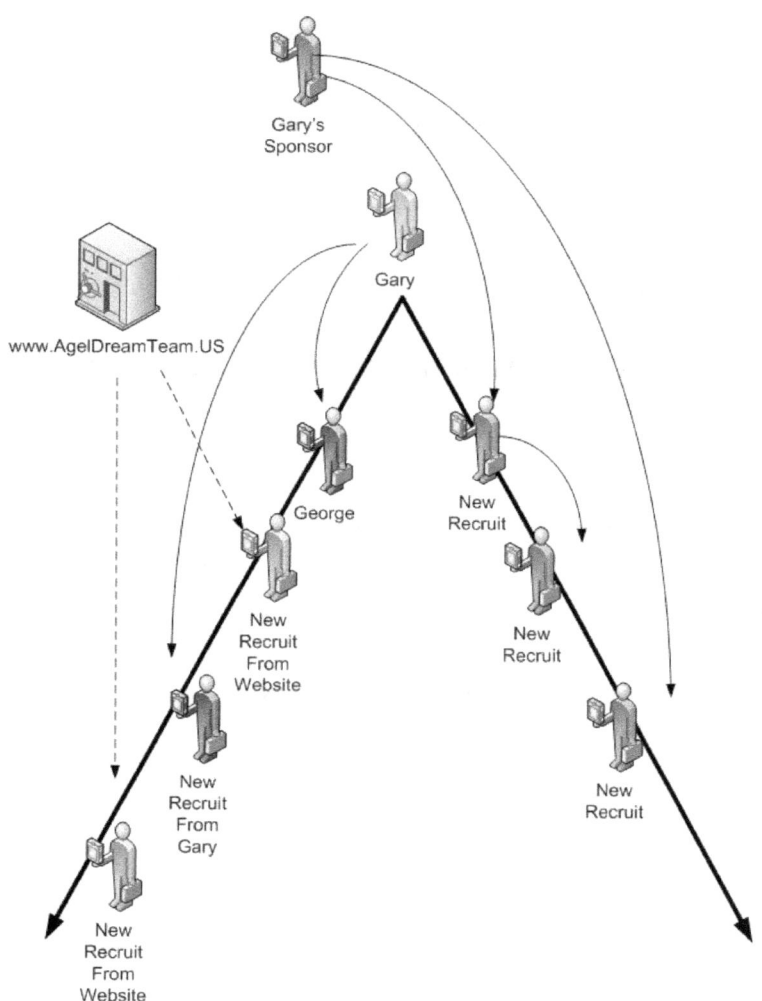

Example of a Power Leg
Accelerator To Grow Your Business

Buying An Existing Organization

GC: One often overlooked option for accelerating your growth and minimizing your initial workload is to purchase an existing network marketing organization from another party.

Sometimes these positions are hot and active, and other times they are inactive (or dormant). Regarding an inactive account, you will need to verify with the company that you can reactivate it or you might find yourself starting at the bottom!

An outright purchase of this fashion will likely be more expensive than the cost of an initial enrollment, but it may be money well spent.

How do you find an existing organization that may be for sale?

Search for the network marketing company of interest to you at eBay, or other online auction sites. Likely, you will find them for sale. I did when I conducted my search.

Joining a Dream Team

What do I mean by joining a DREAM TEAM? Simply put, I mean to ally yourself with proven network marketing professionals that have a track record of past success.

In this way, you will not be going "at it alone" for you can leverage the past experience of these individuals so that you can avoid the common pitfalls. How do you do this? You join a true growth potential network marketing company (like Agel) in its infancy so that you can reap the greatest benefits.

By using this methodology you will be able to model how you conduct your business after those that are considered professionals in the field. This will drastically increase your chances of success.

Why would the experts teach you their proven secrets?

Always remember the greatest axiom of this business model:

If you are successful, then those that have sponsored and trained you will find greater success and compensation for themselves. In other words, it is in their best interest to help you to succeed.

But how do I ally myself with these people that I don't even know?

Simple. True network marketing professionals have used their past successes and failures to create unique training materials that will provide you with all of the insight and guidance that you will need. You can take advantage of these tools to learn the most effective techniques to grow and develop your business.

As a special bonus, you will be able to leverage these same materials to use as training materials for those prospects that you recruit thus solving half of your problems from the very beginning.

X.   Closing Thoughts

GC: In the preceding chapters Gary and I have discussed various techniques that we have used successfully to generate wealth for ourselves and our families. By maintaining the proper mindset and utilizing tested and proven techniques, we have been able to put these strategies to work for us.

 But you may be asking at this point what does it all mean and what will these techniques do for me? The answer is simple:

You Too Can Achieve Financial Freedom

I have personally used these network marketing techniques to generate a business center that averages in excess of $80,000 of sales each and every month.

When I started in network marketing, I truly never dreamed that I would achieve this level of success. I can assure you that I am not a natural-born salesperson, nor do I possess unique insight that allowed me to succeed. I simply used perseverance and an unending willingness to put forth the extra effort to achieve my goals.

Using his techniques for real estate investing and information marketing, Gary has been able to accumulate multiple millions in real estate holdings during the last 5 years.

This may sound too good to be true, but I can assure you that it is true. I will not pretend to give an iron clad guarantee that if you use our techniques that you will achieve the same level of success.

But I can assure you: if you implement these strategies and those explored further in our *Agelations Home Study Course* and our monthly newsletter, *The Profiteer,* you will definitely have an edge.

We can and will serve as your guide to give you your best opportunity to find success. We have provided the framework; the rest is up to you.

Thank you for spending this time with us. Gary and I each hope that the contents of this book will open your eyes to some of the tremendous potential that exists in the world today for generating additional sources of income.

Here's to YOUR next million bucks!

With warm regards, we are,
Gary Lee Vincent & George Cunningham

Index

Y

Resources

HomeBizMarketeer

AGELITY INC.

If you are interested in learning more about the ways and means to implement the business strategies that we have discussed, please feel free to visit the following website:

HomeBizMarketeer.com

To subscribe to *The Profiteer,* visit:

HomeBizMarketeer.com/Profiteer

A sample of the newsletter can be downloaded for inspection.

Agel

To learn more about the tremendous opportunity provided by becoming an Agel Team Member then go to our site at:

www.AgelDreamTeam.US

Burning Bulb Publishing

www.BurningBulbPublishing.com

- *The Winner, The Loser: The Story Of My Life At 21*
- *Agelations: Unlocking the Secret Strategies of the Rich to Help You Succeed in Business and in Life*
- *Agelations Home Study Course*
- *Passageway*

Vincent Record Company

www.GaryVincent.com

- *100 Percent*
- *Passion, Pleasure, & Pain*
- *Somewhere Down The Road*

CONGRATULATIONS!!!

"Your Purchase of *AGELATIONS* entitles you to receive \$50 off the *AGELATIONS HOME STUDY COURSE* and as an added BONUS, one free month of *THE PROFITEER*, the monthly business newsletter from HOMEBIZMARKETEER.COM: a combined \$85 value!"

Dear Innovative Entrepreneur,

By reading AGELATIONS, you have taken the first step down a path that will lead to SUCCESS in the 3 most exciting, profitable, and innovative business opportunities available today:

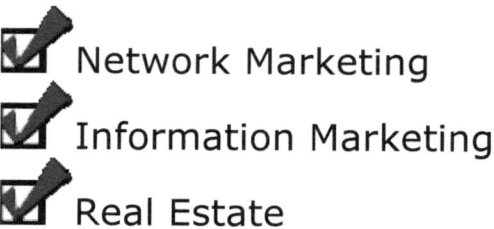 Network Marketing

Information Marketing

Real Estate

NETWORK MARKETING!!!

Learn how to become a network marketing PRO and have prospects standing in line to work with YOU.

Learn the PITFALLS to avoid and the PROVEN techniques that have been used to create down-lines generating tens of thousands of dollars in sales each month.

In the **AGELATIONS HOME STUDY COURSE** and the pages of **THE PROFITEER**, you will learn the innovative techniques used to build LEGACY positions in network marketing by using both the Internet and the traditional word-of-mouth approach.

VISIT
www.HomeBizMarketeer.com
TODAY!

INFORMATION MARKETING!!!
Learn how to become an information GURU!

MASTER the techniques needed to create multiple **INCOME** streams from your own home using your own creativity and at an **UNBELIEVABLY LOW COST.**

At **HomeBizMarketeer.com**, we offer solutions that will get you out of the cubicle, the rat race, and will allow you to become your OWN BOSS.

No other opportunity offers the enormous benefits provided by Information Marketing and the Internet.

Get your copy of the AGELATIONS HOME STUDY COURSE to begin your journey into a more PROSPEROUS and FULLFILLING future.

REAL ESTATE INVESTING!!!

Real Estate Investing is the most proven wealth building formula that exists.

Learn how to:

Buy and sell houses.

Buy tax liens and tax deeds.

Build, purchase, and operate self storage facilities.

And MUCH, MUCH, more.

In the **AGELATIONS HOME STUDY COURSE**, you will find honest, straight forward, and easily understood techniques that will empower you to SUCCEED.

We stand behind our products and offer full money-back guarantees if you are not completely satisfied.

VISIT

www.HomeBizMarketeer.com/Agelations

To get your copy of the
Agelations Home Study Course.

Discount Certificate

Save $50.00 off the purchase of the
Agelations Home Study Course

Visit

www.HomeBizMarketeer.com/Agelations

Enter Discount Code
J2W69HUR
at checkout

QUICK ORDER FORM

Email Orders: Orders@BurningBulbPublishing.com

Fax Orders: 270-477-4512

Web Orders: BurningBulbPublishing.com (click "Titles")

Postal Orders: Burning Bulb Publishing, P.O. Box 4721, Bridgeport, WV 26330-4721

Please send the following books:

_____

_____

_____

Name:_____

Address:_____

City:_____State:_____Zip:_____

Telephone:_____

Email Address:_____

Shipping:
U.S.: $4.00 for first book and $2.00 for each additional product.